Mentoring *for an* Audience *of* One

Acclaim for
MENTORING FOR AN AUDIENCE OF ONE
from students of the training seminar "Biblical Mentoring"

"The very, very best! Awesome. Knowledge expert, technically and biblically sound. Truly an anointed man of God. . . ."

"Dr. Oakes speaks from experience where he has allowed God to produce godly wisdom in him that he in turn is able to give his audience. Very simple and down to earth—straight from the heart."

"This program has given me the tools to be confident in stepping out and assuming the leadership roles I am being given. I am excited!"

"Dr. Oakes is an extremely well-rooted, strong man of God with a sincere, loving heart. This is a humble man with a definite anointing to mentor and train others to mentor."

"I've learned that mentoring is the core, the cell, and the life of the church."

"This material made a tremendous impact on me, and I will be absorbing it for some time. It made connections for me, gave me new concepts, helped me see my relationship to God differently, and also how free I am to follow Him."

"This material spoke especially to my heart and clarified more how I am to move toward my purpose and calling. It helped me to understand more how the Holy Spirit works in my life."

"Leadership must be receptive to the principles taught here, for the body of Christ needs mentors."

"Dr. Oakes knows how to stir the hunger in all of us to reach out to the Father. What a blessing and much appreciated."

Mentoring *for an* Audience *of* One

A Call for Purity
of Motive and Practice

CHARLES G. OAKES

PROVIDENCE HOUSE PUBLISHERS
Franklin, Tennessee

Printed in the United States of America

0 5   0 4   0 3   0 2   0 1   1   2   3   4   5

Library of Congress Catalog Card Number: 2001086170

ISBN: 1-57736-207-1

Cover design by Gary Bozeman

PROVIDENCE HOUSE PUBLISHERS
238 Seaboard Lane • Franklin, Tennessee 37067
800-321-5692
www.providencehouse.com

I send greetings to the noble mentors
trained in the principles found here,
who have partnered with the Father
in behalf of mentorees here and abroad
to assist in the perfecting
of their divinely bestowed purposes.
Your example has led to yet
new generations of mentors.
You are foundational in your efforts,
and I salute you.

CONTENTS

Foreword   xi
Preface & Acknowledgments   xiii

Introduction   Quo Vadis Mentor?   xvii
    Why Do We Mentor? xviii • Why Another Book on
    Mentoring xxii • Conclusion xxxiv •

PART I   A Theology of Mentoring   1

1. The Audience of One   3
    A Radical Approach 5 • Ways to Fellowship with God 8 •
    Conclusion 18 •
2. Mentoring from a Kingdom Perspective   21
    Understanding the Kingdom 21 • Contrasting the Church
    and Kingdom 26 •
3. Biblical Principles of Mentoring   33
    The Principles and Responsibilities 33 •
4. Calling, Purpose, and Destiny   51
    The Marketing of Success 52 • Calling and Purpose 53 •
    The Nature of Inheritance 59 • Learning of Bestowed
    Value 65 •
5. Transitions in Mentoree Growth 1: Personal and
    Interpersonal Changes   69
    Personal History as Foundation for Growth 69 • Disciples:
    The Raw Material of Mentoring 71 • Graduation from
    Discipling 72 • Transitions during Mentoring 74 •

6. Transitions in Mentoree Growth 2: The Emotions of
   Change   83
   The Emotions   83 • Conclusion   97 • Postscript on Figure 1
   97•

PART II   Special Applications to Leadership and
                 the Marketplace   99

7. Mentoring Future Leaders   101
   Leadership in the Bible   102 • Current Leadership
   Patterns   104 • The Models of Leadership   106 •
   Leadership Development and Deployment   110 •
8. Mentoring for the Marketplace   115
   Learning by Experience   116 • A Biblical Understanding of
   the Marketplace   118 • The Ultimate Vision   131 •

PART III   Managing the Mentor Program   133

9. Choosing the Mentoree and the Mentor   135
   Choosing the Mentorees   135 • Who Mentors?   138 •
   Matching Mentor and Mentoree   140 • Atypical Mentorees
   and Mentors   144 •
10. The Sponsoring Organization   151
   Biblical Vision   153 • Church Structure   155 • Structure
   as *Nomos*, *Eros*, and *Agape*   157 • Where in the Organization
   Does Mentoring Fit?   161 •
11. Implementing the Mentoring Program   165
   Preprogram Development   165 • Program Development
   167 •

Epilogue   Eulogy to a Purpose-Driven Life   175
Appendix   Annotated Glossary on Types of Influence   176

                 PerfectingPurpose™   182
                 Notes   183
                 Bibliography   188
                 About the Author   190

Figures

1.   The Mentoring Journey   86
2.   Four Dimensions of the Visionary Leader   106
3.   Matching Mentoree and Mentor   142
4.   Mentoring's Triadic Relationship   144
5.   Mentoring Development Process   168

FOREWORD

MENTORING, LIKE LEADERSHIP, IS TODAY'S, AND MOST PROBABLY TOMORROW'S, HOT TOPIC. YOUR READING OF THIS FOREWORD SAYS SOMETHING ABOUT YOUR INTEREST IN OR CONCERN ABOUT mentoring and its role in producing leaders. You may be a church or parachurch leader and long to see God's people (yourself included) more spiritually mature so they might use their giftedness and help others do the same. If so, you have chosen the right book.

I met Charles Oakes in the late 1950s at the University of California-Berkeley, where for a brief time we served Christ together in student ministry. He is a friend of many years, and I deeply appreciate his friendship and passion for Christ's ministry. In this book, he combines both the theoretical basis for mentoring and the very practical tools for developing a mentoring ministry, particularly a church-wide mentoring program. His treatment of institutional mentoring is especially useful as he examines methodology and its motives in the light of biblical truth.

Oakes writes to ministry leaders and mentors who desire to develop or strengthen mentoring both in their own lives and in their ministries. He is passionate about the nurturing and growth of followers of Christ. He is not simply a theoretician. His words derive from extensive experience as a behavioral scientist and management consultant and out of wide-ranging acquaintance with the issues of mentoring. He draws liberally from psychology, leadership, sociology, theology, literature, and history. He has developed mentoring programs in businesses and in churches, including the seven-thousand-member church of which he is a lay leader.

Part 1 of this book provides a biblical basis for mentoring and, importantly, why mentoring must be responsive to the Audience of One, namely Father God. Particularly helpful are two chapters on transitions occurring in a mentoree's life during the mentoring process. In Part 2, Oakes turns to the topic of leadership in the Bible and provides an excellent discussion of mentoring and leadership, leadership models, leadership development, and deploying mentorees into leadership roles in both religious and secular settings. If you are a church leader, Part 3 will be particularly helpful by providing guidelines for the screening, selection, and matching of mentors and mentorees.

If you have wrestled with the question of how to implement a ministry-wide mentoring program, then this book is for you. Oakes sets forth principles for preprogram development and the actual development of a full-scale mentoring program. Of all the books on mentoring in the Christian market, MENTORING FOR AN AUDIENCE OF ONE is unique in this regard. It clearly outlines how to set up such a program.

Many churches do not have an effective mentoring program. Here is a superb guide to help get one started or upgraded to the next level of effectiveness. I urge you to buy and study this book and to implement the principles it sets forth. Any church committed to making mature disciples of Jesus and fulfilling His Great Commission cannot afford to be without this important work!

Gordon M. Klenck
Professor of Leadership Development and Church Planting
International School of Theology
A Ministry of Campus Crusade for Christ
Fontana, California

PREFACE & ACKNOWLEDGMENTS

THIS VOLUME WILL HELP LEADERS OF ORGANIZATIONS INCREASE THE MATURITY OF THOSE THEY LEAD. WRITTEN FROM A BIBLICAL STANDPOINT, IT APPLIES PRIMARILY TO CHURCHES AND OTHER RELIGIOUS organizations and then to secular settings where corporate managers welcome principles of the kind I offer. Another group for whom I write are mentors-in-training. These are not recent arrivals to the Christian walk; rather they have proved themselves ready for training as leaders who will mentor others who seek their purposes in the kingdom of God.

DNA is a modern buzzword. It refers to the personal genetic code that predetermines the course of our biological future. Each Christian, as I will show, inherits a piece of divine DNA from the Creator. This is the raw material of purpose. The Father's plan is that all of His children live out their purposes based on that divine DNA. You may be destined to be a minister or military officer, an evangelist or an electrician, a worship leader or a worker of bronze, a spiritual counselor or a gourmet cook—whatever it is, God has a plan. It is the mentor's task to help identify the plan, factors that may encourage or hinder it, and then guide that growing Christian to any of a million corners of the world. The place may be in the institutional church, the marketplace, the operating suite, the mission field, or some high-energy adventure. When we mentor according to the principles presented here, people come to fuller understanding and practice of their God-given purposes. *What is more, they will be leaders relative to that purpose!*

Some will call part I theoretical or even theological, but it is unbending as a basis for mentoring. Rest assured that this is not some secular model made to look religious by the attachment of Bible verses. Wherever I have mentored or trained mentors using materials found in part I, I have seen revival occur "on the spot." Testimonies to this abound, some found inside the book's cover and others scattered throughout the chapters. The people who enroll in our training programs are not novitiates. All have demonstrated their readiness to serve others. Some of them are pastors with graduate ministry degrees; others are committed laypeople with business and professional backgrounds; and some are skilled in the trades or arts. Together they represent a cross-section of American life. *This is a cross-section with promise, and that should be good news to leaders.*

Those we mentor have successfully completed basic disciple training and have begun to learn correct behavior, character development, and the basic Christian doctrines. They are far from being ready for training as mentors, however. Nevertheless, because of their early faithfulness, they are prepared for the next chapter in their spiritual and natural growth—discovering God's purposes for their lives. Furthermore, this is true irrespective of the age of the person mentored.

The introduction explains why we mentor in the first place and why I wrote this book, considering the many articles and books already on the subject. The short answer lies in the fact that I have discipled and mentored Christians at different stages of maturity for over fifty years. I have learned much during that time, even if sometimes by default and serendipity, and I believe more is required. We need a return to purity of motive and practice. The principles and practices found here are not hypothetical; they have stood the test of time. We have seen life-changing results from among those we prepared to be mentors during the training sessions and then from among those they, in turn, mentored.

In chapter 1, I offer a radical approach to fellowshipping with God. It is the linchpin for MENTORING FOR AN AUDIENCE OF ONE. It is radical because the initiative for that fellowship, and for finding our purposes, is God's and not ours. Chapter 2 challenges whether we mentor to fill institutional church slots or to serve the kingdom. Failing to answer with the latter, or not even venturing to answer at all, is sufficient reason to read further. The materials of these first two chapters have never failed to bring revival during our seminars. When that happens, we stop the session and allow the impacted students to negotiate with God, often with the caring ministry of others gathered around them.

In chapter 3, I present ten hard-core, straightforward principles of mentoring, each with its biblical roots. These principles are important for all relationships, but they are indispensable for mentoring. Chapter 4 discusses the origin of purpose, how we can discover it, and what hinders it. This information acts as a springboard for mentoring in either church-related or secular pursuits. Many trainees experience relief as they discover that the "burn" for secular pursuits that has been smoldering in their inner parts, sometimes for years, can be as much God-given as for those normally reserved for the institutional church.

Chapter 5 is the first of two chapters dedicated to the transitions occurring in the mentoree's life. Here, I cover the personal and interpersonal dynamics of those transitions. Chapter 6 covers the emotions of transitions. This unique topic evaluates emotions from a biblical point of view and recognizes them as useful "road signs" indicating where in the journey of growth the mentorees are. ("Mentoree," "mentee," and "protégé" seem to be interchangeable across mentoring literature. I use "mentoree" in this book and apologize to those who feel I should have chosen one of the others.) Spiritual and behavioral dimensions of growth come together during these transitions. Growth brings pain, disturbs predictable relationships, and clarifies why suffering and obstructions are necessary. Many who have been in the training seminars have experienced freedom from guilt and bondage through these materials. The information and experiences the mentors receive as students is then passed on to those they mentor. Jesus' promise to set captives free is available to believers at any level of maturity.

Part 2 has two practical applications of mentoring. Chapter 7 addresses how we mentor people regarding their leadership potential, an important aspect of which is determining just what style of leadership they have. Chapter 8 answers the question of how to mentor people for the marketplace. After all, this is where most Christians live out their witness. This chapter provides an enlightening perspective that gives hope and a scriptural strategy for making an impact on corporate operations and policy.

My pastor is a loving and visionary man. After fifty years of leading his church from seventy souls to seven thousand, there has never been a church split. He confesses: "I'm no manager; I need others to work out what God tells me we are to do."

Therefore, part 3 is for people like my pastor who delegate management responsibilities to others. Chapter 9 explains the selection and matching of mentors and mentorees; chapter 10 presents the organizational factors that contribute to or hinder program development; and chapter 11 describes the systematic way to start and manage a mentioning program.

The epilogue is a eulogy in behalf of one man's purpose-driven life. Many will see the epilogue as an autobiography they themselves would have written, or, following the precepts in this book, someday intend to write. If so, the epilogue is our gift to you.

Many have justifiably asked how our brand of mentoring differs from a variety of other interpersonal influences such as coaching, counseling, discipling, and teaching. The appendix responds to these questions as an annotated glossary of terms.

I owe debts to those responsible for depositing in me a biblical foundation from which I have had the privilege of making many applications to the affairs of life, including this excursion into biblical mentoring.

In the beginning, four men trained by the Navigators—Jim Leseur, John Coleman, Ken Swan, and Vince Castro—introduced me as a fifteen year old to inductive Bible study and allowed me to sit with them at the feet of Dawson Trotman, the charismatic founder of the "Navs." During my days in the military, Don Rosenberger, an ex-Nav, encouraged me to increase my skills in biblical interpretation, and I will ever be in debt to him. Others have laid various foundational truths. I did not know George Eldon Ladd or Charles Simpson personally, but their expositions cleared the air and settled questions on the kingdom of God, the church as the body of Christ, and the institutional church. Let me say, gentlemen, many have come to God when they learned the difference, and others have found freedom in God because of what I learned from you and then passed on.

One man stands out in influencing my life and this book, and his handprints are evident throughout. From Bob Mumford, I learned "intimacy with the Father." This cemented in me the concept of Audience of One, and that the *agape* road is the only appropriate path to the Father and the only way mentors can self-lessly mentor those in their charge. Bob Mumford never was a mentor to me, but as a model, his influence made its mark and successive generations of mentors will be the beneficiaries.

INTRODUCTION

Quo Vadis Mentor?

THIS INTRODUCTION ANSWERS TWO MAJOR QUESTIONS: WHY MENTOR IN THE FIRST PLACE, AND WHY IS ANOTHER BOOK ON MENTORING NECESSARY? THE FOUNDATIONAL CONCEPT, "MENTORING FOR AN Audience of One," is the critical perspective required for a theology of mentoring that addresses, and sometimes challenges, historical and contemporary trends. Some of these are church-based and others are demographic and global.

"Quo Vadis?" Where are you going? The question is the title of the 1896 novel by Nobel laureate Henryk Sienkiesicz and is the story of a pagan Roman soldier, Vinicius, who courts to be his concubine a stunningly beautiful woman, Ligia, a Christian. Confronting Ligia's intention to live a pure life and then meeting her friends is too much for Vinicius, and the warrior capitulates to a Superior Force and becomes a Christian.

"Quo Vadis Mentor?" I have grappled with this same question. If there is a kind of mentoring that, like Ligia, is a pure representation of Scripture, then this book is an unashamed effort to find it. After spending forty years in the secular marketplace and tasting more than my share of secular approaches to mentoring and others purporting to be Christian, and after spending more than one half of a century exploring the Scriptures for authentic practical theologies, I remain confident we can respond to *"Quo Vadis?"* with "Yes, we do know where we are going." This book charts the course and is a guide for the journey.

WHY DO WE MENTOR?

We mentor because mentoring meets a universal need in humankind. Man seeks purpose. God has a specific purpose for every one of us. The purposes of some are to mentor others to find and perfect their purposes, and we have adopted *PerfectingPurpose*™ as our trademark. In this sense, the mentor is in relationship and partnership with God in behalf of others. It is an intimate triadic relationship.

Many realize as they make their way through life that they exhibit patterns of thought, aspirations, and actions. They meet someone new, and almost as an afterthought, an old friend in the form of familiar conversation, posture, or feelings reemerges. They feel at home with the familiar. They join an organization or get a new job; again, there are familiar patterns. These come under different names—a bent or leaning, one's lot, a calling, a gift of grace, an inclination, a divine purpose, or destiny. As surely as these reappear, time after time, year after year, they are ours. We stake claim to "peculiarly mine" qualities with their recognizable identity. We embellish these with our personal infrastructure—vocabulary, professional pursuits, academic degrees, childhood and adult toys, libraries, recreational activities, vision, mission, destiny, relationships, and even aversions to some relationships. These patterns are evidence of the divine DNA referred to earlier.

The French have a name for these. They call it the *raison d'etre*, or our "reason for being." Pursuit of the *raison d'etre* takes on a life of its own and commands more of our attention. Friends and relatives may say we are driven or that we are compulsive. The French have another term to describe intense pursuits of purpose. It is the *idée fixe*. This is the "eye of the tiger" popularized in the *Rocky* movie series, or the picture on the wall that ever reminds us of who we are and what we must do, or the sprinter's visualization of breaking the tape at the other end of the track. Others refer to their "burn." Here enters our will to survive, to live to the fullest—to the end of our purpose, and to produce and to reproduce ourselves in the lives of others. Purpose lived with intensity leads many to construct the final of all purposes, a legacy.

"Quo Vadis Mentor?" The answer is found when the more mature, and often older, man or woman comes alongside the

younger and less mature person and says, "You feel you have some purpose in life; you are feeling a burn, a sense of urgency? Do you want someone else to assist in refining what that purpose is? Do you want a partner to help show and muster the resources to help discover your reason for being? Do you think I can be that person?"

Biblical mentoring is a means to an end. It is not an end in itself to benefit the mentor, the mentoree, or the institutional church. The Christian's ultimate orientation or focus in life is on God the Father. Jesus said He would show us the Father. When He said, "Follow me," He wasn't talking "born again." "I and the Father are one." "See me, and you will see the Father." To follow Jesus was to arrive in the presence of the Father.

Mentoring for an Audience of One recognizes God-given calling and purpose. The mentor helps the less experienced believer bring these to a level of maturity that will be to the honor and glory of God. Mentoring changes relative to our stage or season of life. Purpose can be age-graded and tied to one's station in life: student, spouse, wage earner, or retiree. Organizations of all types, inclusive of modern corporations, relative to their own needs, will designate some employees to mentor others who eventually will be cross trained to other responsibilities or promoted within the company. Big brother or big sister organizations are committed to budding teenagers in need of a surrogate parent. Elementary and high schools, colleges and universities have mentoring programs to improve students' academic skills.

"Resource management" describes the efforts to optimize company use of human resources—the person's skills, talents, and energy. The Bible calls this stewardship. The Bible describes our production of one hundred fold, fifty fold, or thirty fold. The amount may vary, but the Lord expects a reasonable return on His investment in each of us. Some Bible scholars even suggest that eight of every ten of Jesus' parables had something to do with stewardship and return on investment. Mentoring brings together the mentor's stewardship and the mentoree's responsiveness to it, which is a sign of his or her own stewardship. The younger Christian's potential becomes the cause of the more mature Christian's productivity.

The word "mentor" does not appear in the Bible. It is an inferred concept that I believe goes beyond the more familiar "discipling," as explained below. The Scriptures portray discipling as multileveled. Most church-based discipling programs teach the new or otherwise inexperienced Christian the basics: essential doctrine, requirements of right behavior, and character development. When the church stops with these, however, leaders often attribute further growth to some kind of mysterious chemistry that chooses some for Christian advancement and leaves others out.

Bible-based mentoring is capable of optimizing the growth and maturity of the divine seed of purpose, performance, and placement within the community of God.

Once the usual basic discipling is completed, however, the believer not only is ready to move on, but there is something—the *raison d'etre*—that emerges and urges, demands and cries out to be loosed. Chapter 4 deals with this bent more fully.

Bible-based mentoring is capable of optimizing the growth and maturity of the divine seed of purpose, performance, and placement within the community of God. When seen in this way, it is a key strategy for leadership development in the institutional church.

The analogy of the acorn and the oak tree serves us well in understanding the optimization process. New Christians are like acorns—dropped from the womb of towering branches onto bare autumn ground, covered with leaves, and seeking a crevice in which to nest and await the next episode in their predetermined destinies. The acorn has its own personalized DNA—a genetic code that destines it to become, under proper conditions, a reproducing oak tree. Watering, pruning, cultivating, fertilizing, sometimes transplanting, and weathering the seasons transforms the acorn from one stage of development to another—first the sprout, then the blade, followed by the sapling, and eventually the mature reproducing oak. Will the acorn find its crack in the soil or be planted and die? Will it sprout into a blade? Will it be tended and become a sapling? Will it become a rising presence in its own place with promise to reproduce its own kind? The institutional church benefits from taking a lesson from Mother Nature. Many young believers remain immature and undeveloped, never traversing beyond elemental discipling to become productive Christians in the ways God has determined. In God's economy, we must assume that all acorns—divine DNA intact—are destined to become reproducing oak trees.

As marvelous as potential is, it may, alas, forever remain potential. Chapter 5 describes this as a teleological process. Potential looks in the mirror and sees what exists now. It is understandable that Paul saw imperfectly when he looked in a clouded glass mirror. With David's Psalm 139 in hand (verses 13–16), Paul sensed there was something else. Perhaps this is what he remembered when he wrote his letter to the church at Philippi. In Philippians 3:12 he refers to himself and others in the course of their journey as not yet perfect. Yet in verse 15, implying a completed journey, he refers to those who are perfect. Paul looked through the telescope (in fact the whole discourse makes use of the Greek word from which we get our word telescope), and while standing in the here and now, he caught a glimpse of the "there" and "then" and saw what God saw.

When Paul saw the difference between "being perfected" and "being perfect," he had the rationale for verses 13 and 14, and he was excited and motivated. Consider a paraphrase: "I haven't reached perfection yet. I'm only in the process. I'm on a journey, but I'm going to forget and put aside past mistakes, immaturity, hang-ups, as well as useless accomplishments, and doggedly keep pressing on toward what it was I saw when I looked at my future the way my Father sees it."

The mentor stands alongside the mentoree, seeing what it is that God sees (because that is *his* or *her* calling and purpose in God) and keeps pace with the mentoree, either running down the track alongside him or her or shouting from the sidelines.

This is not another book on success motivation, despite suggestions to the contrary. Nor is it positive mental attitude, PMA, with verses attached. My intent is not to provide formulas on how to reach a destiny of our own design and making. Neither is self-realization nor self-esteem my aim. My focus is not at all on self but on God the Father. He is our source; He is the giver of our *raison d'etre* and our *idée fixe*. He is the origin of our divine DNA. In Him is total universal all-encompassing purpose, sufficient for all His children, depriving none. Paul hinted in Ephesians 1:18 that the Father intends each of us to know and experience the portion of our purposeful inheritance that derives from Christ Himself. In ancient Israel, mentors played a significant role in preparing each generation to take its place in the next generation. Resting on the seasoned shoulders of today's mentors is the stability and continuity of the culture and the unfolding kingdom of God.

WHY ANOTHER BOOK ON MENTORING?

The Internet's "Open Text List" recently referenced over 2,300 web sites with information about mentoring. Listed were target populations such as K–12 school programs, higher education, minorities, the military, business, government, industry, trade associations, and others. The list grows proportional to the thousands of new web sites added daily. Early in 1998, the Internet bookseller Amazon.com cited over 18,000 publications, organizations, management forums, seminars, and conferences entirely or in part dealing with mentoring.

The variations on the theme of mentoring are vast. Despite all that has been written, two factors establish how mentoring will uniquely fit into the life of the twenty-first century church. First, the presence of new historical and contemporary trends warrants the need for constant updating. Second, the trends themselves cry out for a radical approach, not unlike the Reformation, that both returns us to theological roots and advances our attention to the prognostications of both Christian and secular futurists. Seven reasons justify this book.

Thirty-Five Centuries of Biblical Precedents

The Old Testament contains many examples from which we infer mentoring relationships. Jethro mentored Moses on how to shepherd sheep and later counseled Moses about delegation of authority. Elijah mentored Elisha about the demanding role of prophet. Naomi instructed Ruth on the cultural intricacies that would appeal to her kinsman Boaz to win him as a husband. Samuel instituted the school of the prophets and began a mentoring effort that lasted generations to the present. Nathan the prophet counseled David, including in-the-face mentoring when dealing with his private sin. Mordecai mentored Queen Esther on how she should appeal to King Ahasuerus and thereby save a nation from extermination. Most assuredly, if ever there was a mainstay of social stability and continuity in Israeli society equal to that of the Old Testament elder, it was the mentor.

Jesus discipled the Twelve, but He singled out Peter, James, and John for special attention—entrusting to them care of His mother, inviting them on the trek to the Mount of Transfiguration and later to Gethsemane, and healing Peter's mother-in-law. Paul oversaw Timothy and Titus and took advantage of his close relationship with Philemon whom he instructed in behalf of his runaway slave, Onesimus. Barnabas instructed Paul on how to present himself to the Council at Jerusalem. He later discipled and then mentored John Mark for about sixteen years. Priscilla and Aquila took Apollos aside and better informed him of essential doctrine. Paul taught Timothy how to identify faithful men, draw them close to himself, and teach them leadership roles in the first-century churches. Peter instructed fellow elders to oversee and shepherd the souls of believers. All of these relationships went beyond what today is known as discipling. The magnitude of their historical significance says much about the shoulders on which we stand.

I often am asked where the mentor fits in the institutional church, and I remind my inquisitors of the countless men and women of the Old Testament in whom God had made a deposit that was passed from generation to generation. This continued in the New Testament church. Not all would carry the titles of pastor, prophet, and teacher, or even elder and deacon, but many men and women of caliber similar to those who had been ordained would mentor to maturity others whom God had called and endowed with divine purpose.

It is a divine calling to be a mentor, and, as we shall see, their importance and need in contemporary Western culture has not diminished. If one needs a title for them, let us try "a pastoring elder without portfolio."

The Prevalence of Secular Models

Older Freudian psychoanalysts mentored each generation of neophytes who happily traced their lineage back to Sigmund Freud. Trade associations assign mentoring roles to older members to orient new members on how to "network the system." Industry leaders often make themselves available to promising "rising stars." Fathers, uncles, and older brothers for thousands of years have mentored younger members of the family. This assured the perpetuity of the family business. Apprenticeships passed down from generation to generation provided name identity and established one's place within the community. Older experts mentored medieval apprentices belonging to the same trade or guild.

Mentoring aggressively entered corporate America in the late 1970s to promote employees from within the ranks, to provide long-term stability of existing structures, and to assure the perpetuation of the corporate ethos. Corporate America embraces mentoring in order to give stability to its structure and provide for the continuity of vision and mission. Corporations accomplish their purposes by being self-serving, and one should not expect it to be otherwise. Mentors exist for the welfare of the organization. Corporations have led the way in management innovation. Changes then spread to others—government agencies, voluntary organizations, foundations, youth and other social service organizations, and public and private education. The institutional church incorporates innovation into its management and operations long after it is in vogue in other organizations.

Mentorism has now evolved into a veritable social movement. There are associations of mentors and joiners seeking to acquire mentoring skills; societies of mentor consultants; national registries in America and abroad and affiliated networks of organizations that provide mentoring; and training programs at institutions of higher learning.

The different expressions of mentoring are so great that wise religious leaders will examine them critically to see if they merit use in organizations that are Christian in principle and practice. This, alas, is not always the case. Uncritical adaptation of secular models to Christian settings deserves the accusation that, once more, the sacred and profane come together in a condition called *syncretism*.

Syncretism: The Problem of Mixture

The history of the church in many respects is equal to Israel's vacillation between devotion to Jehovah and a pantheon of heathen deities. Our history offers a mixed picture of the church's orthodoxy and its inclination to adapt to society's values and adopt secular models of management. The prevalence of mentoring in the secular marketplace makes it a ready model for adoption in the churches, particularly because of similarities between mentoring and the pastoral ministry. All management strategies have underlying ethical or moral implications. Organized religion's tendency to adopt ready-made secular models, therefore, makes it susceptible to mixture, or syncretism.

A simple experiment illustrates the meaning of this fifteen-dollar word. Take a jar and fill it half with water and half with cooking oil. The oil, being lighter, floats and is easily distinguishable from the water. Adding two to three drops of red food dye to the water makes the results more striking, particularly for teenagers whom we always want to impress with a new principle. Shake the jar. Let it stand for a few moments: red water on the bottom, oil on top. The temporary mixing of the two does not represent syncretism, however. Both "systems"—water and oil—retain their integrity although in close proximity to each other. For this illustration, we will label the water "authentic" and the oil as "inauthentic" and a potential corrupter of the authentic. Now for the moment of truth. Add a few drops of detergent to the jar and shake again. Detergent weakens the surface tension of the oil droplets and "makes them feel like water." The oil droplets become indistinguishable from the water and remain in suspension. The water is corrupted. Syncretism refers to the mixing of religious or philosophical beliefs in such a way that the authentic and inauthentic cannot be differentiated. Agents of the Federal Bureau of Investigation learn how to identify counterfeit bills by spending hundreds of hours studying the real ones. Unless the Christian knows the real form of biblical mentoring, how will he or she ever be able to detect the counterfeit? This book has a complicated task: to provide a model of authenticity—to recapture purity of motive and practice.

The secular mentor, steeped in the ways of contemporary management science, is unlikely to know scriptural principles, unless he or she also happens to be a biblically literate Christian. Similarly, the church leader steeped in biblical skills and overwhelmed by clerical duties is not likely to be wise to contemporary secular management science and its underlying ethics, unless, also, he or she comes from a secular background prior to entering ministry. Both can come together—water and oil—ignorant of the other's frame of reference. They commit to a partnership—a marriage of philosophies that is syncretistic in the sum. Technology and new management techniques impress those who are on the outside, pastors included. This is particularly true when fellow Christians recommend them. Many are unwittingly deceived. This need not be the case.

Few would convincingly be able to contest that the institutional church, for its two-thousand-year history, has been more an imitator of its culture than an initiating innovator. Why else did Jehovah repeatedly admonish the Old Testament prophets to warn Israel to mend its ways and avoid mixture?

James Dale Davidson and Lord William Rees-Mogg, writing as economist and historian respectively, describe the expertise with which the Roman Catholic Church upstaged secular political and economic institutions to achieve unprecedented wealth and power.[1] The secret of its success was simple: It incorporated secular philosophy into church practices.

Colonel V. Doner's review of recent church history similarly identifies areas where the church took on the prevailing social ethic in complicity with business leaders.[2] It was weakened in both its testimony and opportunity to be a restorative force between the North and South prior to the Civil War. Later, having incorporated the revisionist theology of the day, the church was defenseless from the onslaught of Freudian psychology, Darwinian evolution, Marxian sociology, and Dewey's laissez-faire educational theories. All found their way into theology and official church literature and programs.

Herbert Schlossberg has given attention to the conflict between Christian faith and American culture, and the influence of the latter on the former.[3] Early twentieth century theologians Paul Tillich and Rudolph Bultmann, explains Schlossberg, advocated that the church engage a process called *correlation,* adapting itself to the values of the society in which it lives. To do so would bring to completion the impact of the emancipated individualism of the Renaissance and the rationalism and naturalism of the Enlightenment on the church and result in what came to be known in theological circles as modernism.

Donald W. McCullough, president and professor of theology and preaching at San Francisco Theological Seminary, adds to Doner's and Schlossberg's research. The church has absorbed numerous economic, social, political, and pop-psychological life-forms of secular society and sanctified them as part of everyday religious experience.[4] Examples from this pantheon of trivial gods include god of my (political, social, or economic) cause, god of my (doctrinal and scriptural) understanding, and god of my (unique, emotional, and spiritual) experience. From the temple of idols, McCullough includes gods of my comfort, my success, and my nation. They have become strategic in making the church a "familiar and comfortable" place in which to listen and worship. The counterfeit easily corrupts the authentic.

Postmodernism since the 1960s has replaced the earlier prominence of modernism. Added to individualism and self-sufficiency are Gnostic spiritualism and mysticism. These influence both religious practice and biblical interpretation: "What I feel the meaning is, is alright; what I feel God is saying to me (because of this feeling I have inside me) is more important than the written Word and, for that matter, what makes you think you are more right than I am?" The advent of feeling, mysticism, spiritualism, and the preference given to emotions should come as no surprise. The New Age movement attached itself to the tails of the modern Pentecostal movement. Once there was sensitivity to things of the Holy Spirit and the "mystical" fruit of the Spirit, New Age religions easily co-opted the church pews.

The church has absorbed numerous economic, social, political, and pop-psychological life-forms of secular society and sanctified them as part of everyday religious experience.

The contemporary church has yet to devise an effective strategy against postmodernism's influences among congregations. After all, modernism itself has yet to be sufficiently rooted out from behind pulpits, Sunday school lecterns, official denominational literature, religious conferences, and, notably, many seminaries. Postmodernism has been one of the most frequent issues we have had to address among our mentorees under the age of thirty. There inevitably was a delay in mentoring until it was dealt with. Can we learn to sufficiently tell the differences so that we can eat the corn and spit out the gravel?

Shifting Church Organization

The Lord gave gifts to the church in the form of apostles, prophets, evangelists, pastors, and teachers (Eph. 4). These positions emerged out of each person's God-given gifts. From among the congregations came new generations of apostles, prophets, evangelists, pastors, and teachers who had been instructed by their predecessors. Others served as elders overseeing the flock of God. Some were deacons who were highly skilled managers or administrative assistants. Elders identified, oriented, and ordained new elders to their responsibilities. The contemporary model for mentoring began with the pastoral ministry. It now is a form of leadership committed to any believer's pursuit, religious and secular alike, taking into account God's purpose-specific investment in a believer's life.

The church's growing interest in mentoring represents a paradigm shift away from traditional ways of accomplishing the goals of the pastoral ministry that concentrated leadership and singular authority at or near the top of an organizational pyramid. This model emerged with the Roman Catholic Church around A.D. 300 and continued in the mainline denominations following the Reformation. Our forefathers Luther and Calvin and others since may have corrected our doctrine, but hierarchy and centralized leadership remained largely untouched.

George Gilder describes a three-step process that helps us to understand changing structures. First, there is a weakening or shortage of traditional roles. Second, there is the rise of different ways to address the inadequacies or shortages of traditional roles. Third, innovative leaders choose from new forms of abundance to redress emergent shortages.[5] Gilder's model is applicable to the paradigm shift within the church.

There is a lessening of pastors committed to the training, oversight, and maturation of the saints. Where biblically functioning elders are present, the pastoral role is somewhat expanded. Where elders are absent or fail to function in a biblical way, on the other hand, pastoral scarcity increases. This helps to explain the increasing number of "burned-out" pastors.

A new abundance of pastoring persons appears in the form of mentors. These have the potential for filling the gaps in pastoral scarcities. Along with the increasing acceptance of mentors, there is new evidence that church counseling programs are beginning to decentralize (something I address more fully in the appendix). Rather than vesting the sole right to counsel in the hands of a few credentialed counselors, the privilege is expanding to include others who connect with people in need of the support of the functioning body of Christ.

In church after church, the cry of dedicated pastors is not "where do I find more time?" but rather "how do I bring my more mature members to the point where they can become an extension of myself?" No clearly defined rules on how to ordain more pastors exist. In some denominations there is an aversion to the post of elder; church counseling programs traditionally were committed to crisis intervention and not to the maturation of the saints; pulpit preaching and lectern teaching transmit information, some enlightenment, and degrees of motivation. Long-term growth, however, requires different strategies than those that are primarily didactic.

Jack Hayford offers a standard for all men to step forward in God's service, to become pastors within the local church by first developing a deeper, more compassionate fellowship with Christ. Hayford encourages the expansion of the pastoring role by mentoring men to cultivate God's promise of fruitfulness as a shepherd—a delegation of authority to mature men who will shepherd others.[6] He remains loyal to traditional terms and forms, although his approach is consistent with one that trains mentors to pastor on a one-to-one basis. Charles Simpson, anticipating the message of chapter 4, made a similar appeal based on years of successful ministry. He writes: "The notion that a person is called simply to be a professional in the life of the church does not exist in Scripture. The biblical call is not to profession but to *purpose*. . . . Only people who know their calling and purpose can say whether they achieve it or not. . . . A major task of leaders is to give their people a sense of purpose. People are happiest and healthiest when living for purpose beyond themselves."[7] Both of these world leaders have led the way in instituting mentoring-type leaders in their churches without emphasizing it as mentoring.

Seen from the standpoint of the larger society, decentralization of the pastoral role is occurring at a time when secular corporate structures themselves are becoming flatter with delegation of authority and encouragement of creativity all the way down to the assembly line. The upcoming generation of lay leaders in churches will come from these "flatter" hierarchies, and elsewhere in this introduction, I address the expectation of Baby Boomers of having a place at the decision-making table.

Restoration of the Saints

The forces that provoke the aforementioned paradigm shift among church leadership derive partly from the church's own doing. Numerous events demonstrate the efforts to restore the saints. One is a growing prayer network: prayer summits, concerts of prayer, citywide gatherings of pastors from different denominations, national days of prayer and fasting, youths united on school campuses around flag poles, prayer marches, congressional and White House prayer breakfasts, and stadium rallies seeking the restoration of families, churches, cities and nations.

Another force demanding a response by the church is the increasing incidence of deviant behavior within the church similar in type and proportion to that found in the non-churched world. Efforts abound to lasso and rein wayward members back into the fellowship of believers. Promise Keepers is only one, although among the more significant, of efforts to restore the role of husband and father to families. Critical to its long-term success are one-on-one mentoring, peer mentoring, and accountability groups.

Promise Keepers prepared for the follow-up to its rallies by conducting mentoring workshops led by consultants Bobb Biehl[8] and father and son team Howard and William Hendricks.[9] The enduring success of Promise Keepers, some say, is not another rally but its efforts to integrate its success through ongoing mentoring into local churches.

Demographic Trends

Demographic trends exist side by side with ethical and moral trends. The generations have beliefs and values unique to themselves. These values sometimes clash and challenge religious leaders whose congregations have a diverse age composition.

Three generations worthy of our attention are the Baby Boomers, their offspring know as Generation X, and retirees and pre-retirees. The Baby Boomers were born between 1946 and 1964. This generation is perhaps the most sophisticated, educated, affluent, and influential generation of American history. This is the "have it all" generation, according to Mike Bellah.[10] Boomers have also tasted of corporate America's secular mentoring. They present three challenges to the church and to the church's mentoring programs.

First, Boomers can detect mentoring syncretism more quickly than many pastors can. Why should self-aggrandizing mentoring, to the extent it exists in the church, be attractive to Boomers who already know all the little corporate tricks? When they make the connection, assuming they are seeking an authentic gospel, they will likely seek out those churches that hold to a line of biblical authenticity. Second, Boomers who discovered the fallacies of their own generation will seek a reality in Christ that will surprise and challenge the most skilled church leaders. Last, Boomers, who first turned age fifty in 1997, are becoming church leaders today, and they are the upcoming generation of older adults. One Boomer, trained as a mentor, was on the local church board. Once he had grasped the essence of the Audience of One for himself, he remarked, "There is something grossly wrong with some of the decisions the board is making. Is this really the church?"

Evangelist Mario Murillo urged the current generation of older Christian adults who had experienced the Charismatic Renewal of the 1960s and beyond to seek a new fire for service to the second group of concern to us—those that Murillo called the "X Generation."[11] Generation X is loosely defined as those born between 1965 and 1981. They are the main practitioners of post-modernism. They are sensitive to the things of the spirit world. Their pre-teen Dungeons and Dragons games wooed them to seek adult versions of religious expression, which makes them a veritable mission field. They wait to be converted, discipled, and mentored. John Seel calls Generation X "neopagans who integrate elements of pantheism, subjectivity, witchcraft and Wicca, the celebration of diversity, and a host of other beliefs."[12] Neopagans as a whole are indistinguishable from others in their age group. They are essentially user-friendly, intrinsically spiritual, and similar to affluent New Agers of the generation preceding them. They have rejected the secular hedonistic culture of the Baby Boomers and the Enlightenment humanism of their parents. They are on the prowl for something to fill that "God-shaped hole in the soul" that makes them warm to relationships and authentic gospel. Studies indicate that while Neopagans reject the authority of their parents—the Baby Boomers—they are more likely to be attracted to those in the Builder Generation who today are grandparents.

The third age group, the Builder Generation, is composed of the elderly. They are the fastest growing group in America. There are thirty-three million people over sixty-five years of age and growing, and many are believers who still have their best music in them. For too long the church has age-graded and separated people by age, similar to the way secular society has. Proportionally, the elderly comprise 13 percent of the population at large, but they make up 20 to 25 percent of most congregations. An uncritical acceptance of secular stereotypes about the elderly has made the church one of the most non-biblical organizations in regards to how it defines and ministers to older adults. Until quite recently a common stereotype was that one resigns to inactivity and is brain-dead at age sixty-five. As a group, older members have remarkable resources, such as surplus and discretionary time, well-developed networks, accumulated wisdom, and a hidden, unrealized desire and burn to lead others to that Audience of One.

An uncritical acceptance of secular stereotypes about the elderly has made the church one of the most non-biblical organizations on how they define and minister to older adults.

Chapter 9 has much to say about the role of the elderly as mentors. Historically, older adults outnumber other age groups among those who mentor, something I have documented in *Working the Gray Zone* (Providence House Publishers, 2000). That book provides readers with a programmed approach to training older adults as mentors.

Global Man and the Global Community

Doug was going with his family to a Muslim nation where Christian literature was taboo. He would be there two years working for an American company. He asked that I mentor him on how to be a better father and husband. On a trip to a Pacific Rim nation where I had traveled on business, a national attached to the American embassy asked that I mentor her to find her God-given purpose in life. For several months, I transmitted via the Internet to Doug and the embassy official. After each transmission, they would respond.

The director of a large missionary organization learned that some of our older mentors were computer literate. I explained that they were capable of providing spiritual support and technical assistance by e-mail. He immediately asked that we meet and discuss a joint effort.

Three businessmen, one on the West Coast, another on the East Coast, and the third in the Southeast developed long distance mentor/mentoree relationships. Distance and time were of no consequence. Community and body life prospered via fax transmissions and cyberspace.

MIT futurist Nicholas Negroponte forecasts a nation "connected" by cyberspace that is becoming a veritable communications gold mine for the elderly.[13] Numerous members of the American Association of Retired Persons have formed a virtual community by e-mail. Forecasters like George Barna feel that up to 20 percent of the population by the year 2010 will be getting their religious and spiritual nourishment by the Internet.[14]

New Age futurists John Naisbitt and Patricia Aburdene in their version of the coming age tell of global telecommunications, the triumph of the individual, and the religious revival of the Third Millennium.[15] There will be too many exciting opportunities for Baby Boomers to surf on the web from church to church.

Davidson and Rees-Mogg (mentioned previously) also forecast that individuals will gain more autonomy in a cyberspace world, and morality will make a comeback. Translated, this means individuals will have a greater moral impact through cyberspace. This cannot be lost when planning the long-term goals of mentoring programs. More church members will become missionaries via the worldwide web and e-mail.

World-class management guru Peter F. Drucker wrote that the "next century already is here, indeed that we are well advanced into it."[16] Drucker's thesis was that technology, while capable of being seen as having a reality of its own, really is an extension of man, and in this way defines and redefines who man is. It is not about tools; it is about how man works. The essence of technology is not so much a question of what the inventor had in mind but how the individual perceives himself when technology is an extension of his being.

This brief excursion with the futurists, were it not that their earlier prognostications already were proving true, may be

construed as superfluous in an essay on mentoring and particularly biblical mentoring. The Christian mentor mentors relative
to the needs, goals, and purposes placed on the mentoree's
platter by a sovereign God. God did this among the ancient
Israelites; He did it among pre-Christian messianic Jews; and He
did it in the church of the first century. There were many cultural
changes in the four thousand pre-Christian years. Change in the
modern era accelerates at a greater rate with each decade; some
say the fund of human knowledge doubles every seven years.
Humankind therefore encounters and perceives the reality
unique to its current era. Each era's reality is a different one and
humans' perceptions follow suit. Still, mentors over the thirty-
five hundred years of their history remained sensitive to the ways
of Jehovah and mentored with a perspective that had permanency to it. Modern global man will benefit from this perspective.

Social, economic, and political institutions are in evolution
and emergence. The Christian remains tied to an unshakable
kingdom. Like Bunyan's Pilgrim, the Christian always is schizoid,
not in a pathological sense certainly, but in the sense he or she
lives in two worlds and two time frames. By God's wisdom, the
mentor constantly weighs, balances, and does the right thing in
behalf of the mentoree. He or she is constrained by an immutable
faith in the context of a mutable world.[17]

CONCLUSION

This summary of trends draws from diverse literature:
management science, the behavioral sciences, wide-ranging
philosophical positions, and the Scriptures. My library liberally
displays both secular and Christian scholars. When diverse
writers begin to report the same message, my spiritual and intellectual antennae awaken and make me take notice.

My interests and concerns are quite simple. The role of
biblical mentoring for the church is to assist in a process where,
through the generations, God has progressively unfolded different
revelations of Himself. This is the stuff of biblical theology. The
mentor on a one-on-one basis works with uniquely crafted people
called to accomplish the Father's time- and space-bound plan.

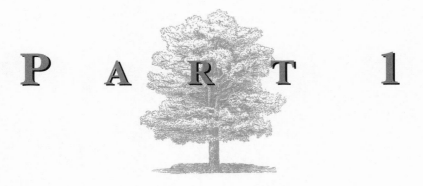

P A R T 1

A THEOLOGY OF MENTORING

CHAPTER ONE

The Audience of One

GOD THE FATHER IS THE AUDIENCE OF ONE. JESUS CAME TO REVEAL THE FATHER, AND HE PROMISED TO TAKE US TO THE FATHER. THE FATHER WAS THE HEARTBEAT FOR ALL THAT JESUS SAID AND DID. SOME writers appropriately say our task as Christians is to be a "Father pleaser." The disciples' obedience to the instructions of Jesus pleased the Father. Our obedience to the written Word pleases the Father.

A *reference group* is a sociological concept. Our families, work groups, play groups, social clubs and special interest societies, fellow students, and, yes, our churches are reference groups. We look at the world through the eyes of our reference groups. Their perspectives are our perspectives; consequently, we are predisposed to see, interpret what we see, and act on what we see from the standpoint of one or more of our reference groups. In one sense, this is good. Reference groups lend a consistency and therefore predictability to how we think and act, particularly for the benefit of others belonging to the same reference group.

Each reference group, again following the sociologists, has in it a few people who are more special to us than others. We all have our favorites. These are our significant others. While the reference group provides us a perspective on life, our significant others are the real champions, heroes, or models for that perspective. It is from these people that we draw the most inspiration and challenge to live the kind of life espoused by the reference group. We watch our significant others closely. We might even put their picture on the wall, on the mirror in the bathroom, or on the door of the refrigerator. We treasure every letter or note we get from them, and if we happen to have elevated them to the level of hero, we save those notes and letters in a special file.

"Whatever I hear my Father say, I say; and whatever I see my Father doing, I do." "I have come to do the will of Him who sent me." With these statements, Jesus declared who His significant other was. Jesus had only one significant other. He loved His disciples; He gave His life for them and for the world. He shared the words of the Father with His friends, but He had only one significant other. His Father was His Audience of One.

Pilate tried to intimidate Jesus. Jesus responded that He could summon legions of angels if He chose to do so and told Pilate to do what he had to. Peter scolded and sought to control the direction of Jesus' ministry when Jesus foretold of His death. Jesus told Peter his statements were of the devil, and He was not the least dissuaded from progressing on toward His destiny. Members of His family tried to get Him to come home and cease all the nonsense about preaching and prophesying. He merely said that those who did the will of the Father were His family and continued about His business. Jesus would not be intimidated or controlled. He knew who He was, where He came from, and where He was going. He came from the Father; He did the will of the Father; He would return to the Father. He really had His act together!

The gospel writers were lavish in their testimony of Jesus' Significant Other (Matt. 7:21; John 5:19, 30; 6:38; 8:28–29; 12:49–50; 14:10). There is no one so disarming and so frustrating to those who seek to control than the person who has centered his or her affection on God the Father! Have you ever met someone who is not for sale, does not have a price, and cannot be intimidated or controlled? It was not that Jesus was His own man; that would have been bad enough. He was God's man, and that insulated Him from any known force, then or now. Please do not get me wrong. I am not suggesting that one's devotion to God should make him or her arrogant or self-sufficient and independent of others. Rather, when our significant other is the Father, as He was for Jesus, then we have our priorities in order and all we do centers around His will for us. It is not that we neglect others, but rather that our ethical system involving others takes its point of departure from the Father.

I left the University of California in 1959 just before the radical student activist movement gained a foothold there. Two years later, I enrolled at Emory University in Atlanta where the "God is dead" doctrine had come into vogue as the new wave of radical theology. Most of us assume when some new idea, ideology, lifestyle, or political philosophy appears out of the pale it is radical. Theological modernism was radical in the earlier years of this century; postmodernism is radical today. If "radical" is new, then neither modernism nor postmodernism is radical, in the sense they represent something new in history. They have existed for a long time, and the challenge of Jehovah to the Israelites throughout the Old Testament to stay the course and remain pure is witness to Solomon's quip that "there is nothing new under the sun."

Noah Webster's definition of radical, on the contrary is, well, radical! Coming from its Latin root, *radix*, it refers to that which proceeds from or pertains to the root or foundation; it is essential, fundamental, and inherently basic. In mathematics, etymology (the history of words), and botany, radicals are first things or principles. In this sense, Martin Luther and John Calvin may not have been reformers as much as they were restorers! Though they are the big movers in the Reformation and Reformed Theology, Luther and Calvin were actually returning to radical first principles.[1]

Mentoring for an Audience of One has roots in a first truth. It is foundational and known to biblically literate Christians and certainly to all Jews. Known as the *Shema*, we find it expressed in Deuteronomy 6:5–6: "Hear, O Israel! The Lord is our God, the Lord is one! And you shall love the Lord with all your heart, and with all your soul, and with all your might." (A complete expression of the *Shema* is found in Numbers 15:37–41 and Deuteronomy 6:4–9; 11:13–21.) This Scripture is of primary creedal importance to the Jews. Young boys, meeting in the homes of their teachers, would read elemental portions of the Scriptures, of which the *Shema* was basic, and from it their faith was established. It also was the radical foundation for Israel's existence, direction, hope, and blessings.[2] Additionally, the *Shema* was the prophetic message the Israelites were to declare to all humankind in all generations. At the heart of mentoring each generation of Jews was the *Shema*.

This carried over to the New Covenant. Jesus learned the *Shema*, and when asked what the greatest commandment in the Law was, He replied by quoting it: "You shall love the Lord your God with all your heart, and with all your soul, and with all your mind. This is the great and foremost commandment. The second is like it, 'You shall love your neighbor as yourself.' On these two commandments depend the whole Law and the Prophets" (Matt. 22:37–40). Again, the *Shema* was central to mentoring in the New Testament church (remembering that the church was birthed before and eventually established the canon of Scripture).

Two aspects of the commandment are important for this discussion. One is the command to have but one God, and the other is to love Him with all our hearts. These are radical and they are the bases for how we mentor.

The Lord Is God: No Other Gods

The *Shema* was the grand center around which the Israelites rallied. As long as they maintained this, they would be a happy, prosperous, fruitful people. When it was let go, all fell into disarray. It distinguished them from all other nations. Wherever they went, their proclamation in and to an idolatrous world was to be "The Lord our God is one Lord."

To perpetuate their commission and guard against mixing their faith with that of heathen religions, Jehovah instructed the Israelites to wear portions of the Scriptures as frontals on their foreheads (Deut. 6:8b). Frontals were religious symbols God had commanded them to wear between their eyes, on their wrists, or attached to the doorposts of their homes. The idea came from the working of livestock (something I learned as a youth on our ranch). Those who work draft animals know the value of frontals, placed peripheral to the eyes or on the bridge of the nose in between both eyes. When the animal looked to the right or to the left, it lost the benefits of stereoscopic or three-dimensional vision. Three-dimensional sight gives animals and man depth perception, or perspective. Assuming that for most readers the Christian community is the primary reference group, then the greater the degree of orthodoxy, the more likely the Father is our preeminent significant other, and the written Word of God gives perspective as we seek to please Him.

Love with All Your Heart

"Having no other gods" is a matter of focus and perspective. "Loving Him with all one's heart" is a matter of intensity and singular affection. The "Hear, O Israel; the Lord our God is one Lord," pressed the people to understand that He was, first and foremost, their God and, secondly, He was to be the center of their affection; they were to love Him with all of their hearts. Here was an invitation to intimacy, and we should not miss its importance.

"Having no other gods" is a matter of focus and perspective. "Loving Him with all one's heart" is a matter of intensity and singular affection.

The word for heart, *leb*, appears 860 times in the Old Testament and describes the inner part of a thing, the inner man, the seat of desire or emotion, the seat of knowledge and wisdom, the memory, the seat of conscience, and the fountain of man's deeds. Probably no other word better summarizes the essence or totality of man. "Heart" describes the depths of the collective soul of the nation. God was urging a national archetype when He invited the Israelites to love Him with all of their hearts.[3]

A Philosophical and Ethical Dilemma

Israel's history was a mixed bag, moving first from fellowship with God, then suffering the consequences of national sin, and eventually returning to repentance, restoration, and fellowship. They failed the test of consistent devotion to God. Understanding the philosophical basis of how Israel then—or any person or group now for that matter—related to God helps explain their cultural dilemma and the ethical bases for personal and national behavior.

One's philosophy of life, comprised of values, the definition of man, and so on, will lay the basis for one's ethics—that is, how the philosophy plays out in behavior and relationships. A valid philosophy is more likely to produce a workable ethical system. If there are flaws in one's philosophy, we can naturally expect there to be problems arising from his or her ethical (that is behavioral) approach to life.

There have been three philosophical and ethical approaches to how humankind has related to God, or, more precisely, how they have sought fellowship with God. I have found that all three ways have penetrated the mentoring enterprise and influenced it for good or for ill. It would be less complicated if each of these different approaches were present in some pure form, each to itself, but unfortunately they get mixed up with each other, and this compounds the problems mentors have in working with mentorees.

WAYS TO FELLOWSHIP WITH GOD

Fundamental religious questions first ask about the ways man seeks to fellowship with God. Greek Hellenism, Judaism, and Christianity, respectively, represent three philosophical systems with ethical implications.

Eros has to do with our desire for heavenly things, *nomos* has to do with fulfillment of the Law, and *agape* deals with God's own love freely bestowed on the sinner. The first two primarily center on man and thus are egocentric and, from God's standpoint, are illegal, while the third centers on God and is theocentric. The Old Testament is the most theocentric of non-Christian beliefs, but put into practice it remained egocentric to the core since its ethic sought righteousness by personal merit. This helps explain the repeated capitulation of the Israelites to sin; they were incapable of living up to the standard of the Law and the expansions of the Law formulated by the priests.

Motif Research

The term *motif* describes these areas of thought. Philip Watson, the translator of Anders Nygren's *Agape and Eros*, described Nygren's book as "motif-research," a method of investigation that seeks to discover the fundamental theme or motive of any given outlook or system of thought.[4] A fundamental motif gives a particular outlook or system its own peculiar character as distinct from all others. The following discussion derives largely from Nygren.

Organizations, like individuals, have prevailing values or themes that are every bit *eros, nomos,* or *agape* and permeate anything they touch, including mentoring. (I further address the manner in which these motifs enter and influence organizations in chapter 10.) The two egocentric motifs reach back into antiquity twenty-three hundred to thirty-four hundred years, and the *agape* motif began with Christ. Because they vie for the loyalty of humankind, they forever are in dynamic tension with each other. They are more than a philosophical triad characterized by détente. In real life, they are mixed. No organization is exempt.[5]

Eros and Mentoring

The classic Hellenistic example of love is Plato's "heavenly *eros*." Man's love for the Divine craves the attractive qualities of its object (hence, the ideas of "erotic" or "eroticism"). *Eros* seeks God as a commodity to satisfy its own spiritual appetite by the possession and enjoyment of Divine perfection. In a word, the person or organization influenced primarily by *eros* does not want God for His sake, but for personal reasons.

Eros, in its most simple form, is self-aggrandizing, self-seeking, and controlling. It longs and strives for what it lacks and needs. The object must therefore have value in order to warrant acquisition. *Eros* gathers, collects, and wants what the other has, and in this sense, jealousy and envy are related sentiments. The tenth commandment was a clear proscription against them: "Do not covet." The desire to acquire and control are the outward expressions of hidden motives to use others for one's own gain and satisfaction. The injunction against organizations and their leaders is not absent from Scripture, as seen in James 2:2–3.

> For if a man comes into your assembly with a gold ring and dressed in fine clothes, and there also comes in a poor man in dirty clothes, and you pay special attention to the one who is wearing the fine clothes, and [with motives of getting a bigger donation from him] you say, "You sit here in a good place," and you say to the poor man, "You stand over there, or sit down by my footstool," have you not made distinctions among yourselves, and have become judges with evil motives [to personally benefit from the rich man]?

James was writing to leaders in New Testament churches. The bishop of Jerusalem, however, was forecasting the same word two thousand years into the future to modern Christendom. We can hardly read such a passage without conviction of *eros* in our own lives. We pray for provision without regard for the Provider. We seek the healing and forget the One who heals. We cry out for peace of soul but are casual and dismissive of the Prince of Peace. Or we seek the emotions and titillating thrill of worship as they tickle our minds and bodies, yet we are oblivious of the Person of God and His majesty.

Mentoring programs that exhibit *eros* have five characteristics which are described below.

Acquisitive desire and longing

Mentoring is used as a means to accumulate and satisfy the desire and longing for prestige, position, reputation, pecuniary gain, acquisition of material possessions, and the emotional or spiritual sense of the Divine and all it provides. All parties to the mentoring enterprise have needs, wants, and desires. A common example is the mentoree who finds a surrogate father, and the mentor who finally finds a surrogate son to replace the one who failed him.

Upward movement to find God

Mentoring ascends to God to receive His provisions and bene-fits ("brownie points"). One new mentoree sat down at the first meeting with her mentoring team and said: "God promised if I delighted in Him, He would give me the desires of my heart, and He hasn't delivered yet, and I'm mad. Can you turn that around for me?" She had yet to learn that biblical mentoring focuses secondarily on the blessing only after there is relationship with the Source of the blessing.

Mentoring mobilizes man's resources to acquire God's purposes, blessings, and destiny. Sponsoring organizations will recruit persons of public reputability, primarily as resources to lend their credentials to the program as the means of assuring success.

Egocentric love

Mentors, in the name of "raising up the next generation of leaders for the church," will recruit, train, and control mentorees to satisfy personal goals. They will acquire a personal following, a mini-church within a church, and achieve personal status to rival other leaders. Mentorees, in the name of "wanting God's best in their lives," will capitalize on the mentor's time. When mentor and mentoree operate in tandem in this way, the relationship is one of codependency.

Search for divine and immortalized life

Mentors seek to establish personal legacies—to immortalize their lives of service in behalf of the next generation of Christians. The mentoree achieves immortality of purpose by seeking historical placement within the kingdom. The sponsoring organization assures its corporate stability and continuity, succession of leadership, and a name of high regard within the Christian community.

Focus on object's value and beauty

The mentor seeks mentorees who are more intelligent, are physically attractive, and show promise. The mentoree chooses mentors who have graduate degrees, are financially and professionally successful, and have the most contacts. The sponsoring organization has its own criteria of desired qualities for choosing mentors and mentorees: education and school attended, ethnic or racial background, place of residence, occupation, athletic ability, physical appearance, age, income, and doctrinal orientation.

Conclusion on the eros motif

Eros is the prevalent motif characterizing the post-modern era and its doctrinal spin-off—postmodern theology. Its affinity for emotion, feeling, and mysticism is tailor-made for Generation X. Members of other generations (in all fairness to Generation X) also succumb to immediate gratification of self. The Baby Boomers certainly have been the most self-gratifying generation in American history, but many of the elderly are not exempt. Social policy has carved out a place for older adults who feel they have paid their dues and earned a place of comfort, ease, and pleasure for the next twenty to thirty years. National organizations exist to cater to older adults given to these values. Although there is much in contemporary society and the contemporary church to appeal to *eros*, we should not let it overwhelm mentoring programs. The prospect of mentoring people in a manner that would perpetuate this devilish fixation on self is a frightening one. (Paul's warning to leaders in 1 Corinthians 3:10–17 should be sufficient cause to take the mentor's task seriously.)

The Charismatic Renewal of the 1960s spawned movements best described by *eros*. Some streams of the renewal catered to humans' natural acquisitiveness and provided a biblical rationale for demanding from God each person's fair share of his or her inheritance in Christ. This is not a commentary on the renewal or the subject streams, per se, other than to note that they lend themselves to an *eros* motive deep in the recesses of man's soul. It is easy to confuse *spirit* with the Spirit. It has not surprised us that large numbers of mentors from these persuasions often end up promising more than they themselves can or God will deliver. Mentorees from the same background enter the mentoring relationship believing it is yet another magic bullet to help them achieve instant promotion, position, and productivity in their place under God's sun.

Nomos and Mentoring

The Christian idea of love points both positively and negatively back to Judaism. The commandment to love God and neighbor is an Old Testament commandment. Despite the love of Jehovah for His people and their expressed love for Him, righteousness by merit sought to placate a potentially angry God. The people felt that the wrath of God in times of peace was distant and slow to burn. Hence, they worshiped idols on the high places, losing sight of judgment until it suddenly came with vengeance. Caught in their sins and shame, they cried for mercy, confessed and repented, received mercy and forgiveness, and, started the cycle all over again by living righteous lives. *Nomos*, in its most simple form, is righteousness by merit and is expressed as legalism.

The *agape* of God in the New Testament was not a new invention reserved for the New Covenant under Christ. God and His character do not change, but the strange effect of the Law on a people yet to experience a "circumcision of heart" left Israel constantly trying to balance their efforts to please God and failing with His judgment, forbearance, and mercy. The problem with *nomos* always has been that humans never can jump high enough to please God. Still, *nomos* has entered into modern Christianity, and we encounter it repeatedly among mentors and mentorees who come from denominations that have four legalistic strands running through them.

Righteousness is by code and observances

Mentoring influenced by *nomos* will be an advanced program designed to orient mentorees to a higher level of righteousness that leads to group acceptance. The codes of righteousness are both proscriptive and prescriptive: some things you shall do; others you shall not—rules of dress, holy day observances, mandatory church attendance, scheduled fasts, and humbling of one's self. The mentor is the arbiter of these.

The inner circle

The choice of mentors depends on their doctrinal and behavioral purity. They are among the elite, the inner circle of the church leadership. Leaders closely monitor them and report in detail on their performance. Similar scrutiny includes mentorees to assure their becoming the next generation of doctrinal and behavioral purists.

We ask church leaders to recommend candidates to our training program. Some come sporting their Sunday school attendance pins on their lapels, showing us their five hundred Scripture memory cards, and proudly exhibiting their ragged paged Bibles—each page underlined and marked in the margins. When these outward evidences are presented as badges of acceptability, we know we have once again encountered *nomos*.

Righteousness spawns invidious comparison

The organization's different strata of righteousness produce a hierarchy given to jealousy and envy. Those in higher echelons possess a "pride of group." Church leaders parade them before the congregation and single them out as worthy of emulation by those not as highly placed. Mentors and mentorees become elite groups and receive diplomas for completing courses. Their vocabulary sets them apart and makes entrance into their circle difficult. Jealousy and envy are relieved in one of two ways: either the envied mentor or mentoree in the inner circle has to quit (which *nomos* does not encourage), or the jealous or envious person has to join the ranks of the envied.

Shame and guilt

The rigorous standards imposed on mentors and mentorees cannot help but produce those who will fail or are in danger of failing. The pressure to perform is too great, and anxiety and paranoia commonly precede the guilt for failing or the shame that results from the exposure of sin. The only remedy is confession before the governing body and repentance for a moral failing. Penance paid assures continued acceptance in the program, restoration to purity, and intensified future adherence to the rules.

Conclusion on the nomos *motif*

Legalism by any name is still legalism, and the resulting bondage is no less today than when Paul wrote his impassioned plea to the Galatians. *Nomos* is a trap. It excludes those who, defined as more deficient in works, are less than righteous. It chokes creativity and only allows for shame and guilt as the fruit of failure. Mentoring that conforms to *nomos* does not liberate the mentorees; rather it inhibits them from pursuing their purposes in God.

Nomos is in those streams of the church known for their legalism. Mentorees coming from these feverishly crowd all waking hours with one church-based activity after another, suggesting that not enough time and energy exist to do "all that God wants me to do." One of the early assignments we give to mentorees is for them to list all their church-based activities. "Why are you so busy? Do you think this impresses God?" An early task of some mentorees is to reevaluate their schedules so they can determine whether they are ready for mentoring.

Agape and Mentoring

The growing fellowship of *agape*-oriented mentors has no problem talking about *agape*. In some respects, we sometimes feel like spectators standing on the sidelines of an athletic contest cheering our team on but not really involved in the competition ourselves. We never said the journey was an easy one. Embracing *agape* (rather, letting it embrace us) takes place while we are still trying to set aside (or be cleansed from) our own *eros* and *nomos*.

We therefore approach this most biblical of mentoring with trepidation and no small amount of humility. We are in the process of learning and reformation. This is a long journey. Our mentorees smile. They watch us learn (and sometimes stumble) as we teach them (and hopefully keep them from stumbling). Mentor and mentoree: both on their respective Pilgrim's Journey.

Agape, as it applies to the purposes of God in our lives, rests on four doctrinal pillars, which we develop shortly. Most readers have learned about four kinds of love in Sunday school: (1) *agape*, or God's sacrificial love, (2) *phileo*, or brotherly love, (3) *storge*, or an earthly father's love, and (4) *eros*, or sexual love. I do not dismiss these, but my purposes are different. I expand significantly on the Sunday school version of *agape* below, and I already have shown the broader implications of *eros*. (Actually, the sexual or sensuous connotation of *eros* as usually presented is quite limited and is more of an "Americanism" than the true Hellenistic definition I use.) Now, to the four pillars.

Agape *is spontaneous and unmotivated*

There are no grounds for *agape* other than in God Himself. His love is altogether spontaneous, and He needs not wait for any stimulus to energize Him to act through *agape*. In relation to man himself, divine love is unmotivated. This is not a commentary on what man is like but rather on what God is like. "But God shows and clearly proves His [own] love for us by the fact that while we were still sinners Christ, the Messiah, the Anointed One, died for us" (Rom. 5:8, The Amplified Bible).

Spontaneous and unmotivated love, having no reason outside of itself, described how Jesus searched for people independent of any value they may have had. Wisdom, strength, or nobility did not awe Him; nor did people of foolishness, weakness, or low regard repulse Him. *Agape* was devoid of ascribing any value to man (1 Cor. 1:26–27), as we see next.

Agape *is indifferent to value*

When Jesus makes the righteous and sinners change places, it first appears He ascribes value to sinners. The German social philosopher Max Scheler came to the conclusion that sinners were "more noble" in the sense they recognize their sin, confess, and repent, and this energized and warranted the *agape* of God. Many make a fetish of this idea, upholding the poor, unattractive, and weak as possessing intrinsic worth. God does not single them out for special favor. No person, regardless of how low he or she has sunk, has more merit than another irrespective of how high he or she has ascended. There is no transvaluation of worth in the scheme of Jesus. The door opened to all (John 1:12; 3:16; Acts 2:21; 10:43). When God loves the sinner, *agape* is the driving force. When God loves the righteous, *agape* is the driving force. Man's sin and righteousness count for nothing. It is only when all thought of man's attributes or their absence is set aside that one can understand what *agape* is. Modern "enlightened" man has lost sight of this kind of sovereignty.

. . . eternal purpose derives not in terms of what the mentoree brings to the table but what he or she finds on the table because God already has put it there.

The central key to mentoring for God's plan in the mentoree's life is that eternal purpose derives not in terms of what the mentoree brings to the table but what he or she finds on the table because God already has put it there. The mentoree reaches down and picks it up and then becomes available to what God wishes to do in his or her life.

Agape *is creative*

One of the most remarkable aspects of *agape* and the deepest reason for its uniqueness is that it is creative love. God loved that which was devoid of value, and that which has no value acquires worth by virtue of His loving it.

My first course in organic chemistry was under Dr. Melvin Calvin, who just a few years before had won the Nobel Prize for discovering the process of photosynthesis. When I first sat down in that class, I knew nothing. There were over a thousand of us sitting in Wheeler Hall on the University of California campus in Berkeley. Dr. Calvin was clear and concise. He took questions from the students. He sometimes stopped and singled out a student and asked if he or she understood the lecture. This went on for weeks. By the time the course was over, Dr. Calvin had conferred value on me in a way I never before had known value. What was the content of that value? The content was Dr. Calvin's deposit in me of his knowledge.

Agape does not recognize value; it creates it! *Agape* is a value-creating principle. Mentorees are surprised when they get undivided attention from the mentor. They see themselves in a new way. They have worth beyond their expectations. Unfortunately, much modern theology, religious pop psychology, and those movements seeking to ascribe to humans some intrinsic, deeply seeded value abuse the value-creating principle. A. Von Harnack, a leading theologian quoted by Anders Nygren, in 1913 ascribed a major theme to the teaching of Jesus which he entitled "God the Father and the infinite value of the human soul." Harnack chose Mark 8:36–37 (KJV) to justify this idea: "For what shall it profit a man, if he shall gain the whole world, and lose his own soul? Or what shall a man give in exchange for his soul?" Harnack's comment, that "all who bear a human face are of more value than the whole world," implied the "infinite value of the soul." This by no means is a central idea of Christianity. It is, however, central to both religious and secular humanism.

The mentoree blessed by *agape* has received a unique piece of the inheritance of Jesus Christ. Mentor is in partnership with the Father to walk alongside the mentoree to bring that inheritance or purpose to the point of fruition. The content of bestowed value is the purpose to which God calls us. He bestows value; purpose emerges from Him. The image-ness with which we were designed and created has become flesh in no less way than Jesus was the Word that became flesh and came to dwell among us.

Conferred value determines our fellowship with God

Value and the purpose that defines it for us now becomes the content of the fellowship God Himself has initiated. Consider the life of David. God loved and bestowed value on David by giving skills in the composition of "praise and music," and David thereby fellowshipped with God in voice and writing through psalms, songs, and spiritual songs. In the mid-twentieth century, Davidic Temple Worship, an element in the Charismatic Renewal, represented a rebirth of David's early life purposes. God loved and bestowed value on David by anointing him to be king, and David thereby approached God with entreaties for the peace of Israel and its protection. When he was but a lad, God bestowed value upon David by giving him the gift of shepherding, out of which came his insights regarding meditation, spiritual growth, and protecting those under his care. Because He loves, God bestows value on His children, and the value—in the form of purpose—becomes the rationale for each child's communion with his or her Father.

One of the most startling revelations the mentoree will have is that the unique gift of purpose that God puts in him or her is the basis for fellowship with the Father. Out of this comes a personal posture that is bold, determined, and not easily dissuaded from the journey.

It is the responsibility of the mentor to appeal to the Father, to see from His perspective what the purposes are for each mentoree, and then to partnership with Him to bring those purposes to maturity in the life of the mentoree.

CONCLUSION

Eros and *nomos*, because they are egocentric, have limits placed on how successful they can be in establishing our fellowship with God. Their limitations become our limitations. Try as *eros* will, it can never satisfy. Our desires, pecuniary and acquisitive inclinations, and possession and control of others are insatiable and have limits. The psychologists agree on this point: There comes a time when even the aroma and gustatory delight of a prime rib roast loses its appeal.

Try as *nomos* will, it can never make righteous. As part of humankind, our righteousness inevitably engulfs us in greater degrees of legalism, enslaving us and those on whom we would impose our rules. The standard increases, and, alas, we fail to make the mark. Guilt takes over, not to be relieved, leaving the legalist in chains of his or her own making. Both *eros* and *nomos* fall short on the grounds of a common and major philosophical flaw that has ethical implications. In desperation, we seek to ascend to a holy transcendent God, when only God is capable of rendering Himself immanent.

Fellowship with God is founded on this initiative. My self-abasement, self-flagellation, meritorious conduct, and repentance are no more able than my righteousness to move God to love me. We conclude, from humankind's perspective and its otherwise illegal efforts, there is no way to reach Him. In this sense, *agape* is revolutionary. Fellowship only happens at His discretion. *Agape* is God's way to us, and the mentoring relationship intensifies this for the mentoree.

The relationship between Jesus and the disciples exemplified the quality of relationship they were to have with the Father. David caught a glimpse of the kind of fellowship that was possible, and he expressed it in Psalm 37:4. A brief discussion on this passage is a fitting conclusion to our discussion on relationship with God, and it prepares for later discussions on our purposeful inheritance in Him.

"Delight yourself in the Lord." "You will receive the desires of your heart." These two statements provide remarkable insight into our search for God's highest. *Delight* is an exceptional word. Several ancient languages have some form of it, which suggests that it held a high place of meaning across cultures. It is a sensuous term, connoting the close intimate embrace by the lover of the beloved. When first learning of this word, I remembered the sculptor Rodin's statue entitled "The Kiss." Two lovers are caught in intimate embrace, with the shape of the beloved yielding to the conformation of the lover. *Delight* is the amorous gesture of the woman, softly and delicately appealing to her lover, while with her supple pliability, she is reshaped to his body.

Significant in my musings on *delight* was the fact that David was the one who was writing, reminiscing on the closeness he felt as he meditated on God. It is important to remember here that God wanted all generations to know that David was a man after His own heart. Did David have this in mind—that "delight" was a joining of two hearts; heartbeats thumping in cadence, blood's life force flowing from Creator to creature and back again? Was this the essence of what Jesus sought to convey to His disciples about fellowship with the Father? Was this the beginning of *agape*? How was this to play out in the mentoring relationship? How would the mentor handle this, as he or she again impressed the mentoree with the significance of an Audience of One?

Psalm 37:4 is one of the most misused passages of Scripture. Selfish, self-aggrandizing people, avarice pounding in their breasts, incriminate themselves when they turn "And you shall have the desires of your heart" to their own purposes. Prostituted (read *eros*) religion is that way. It holds out a promise to the seeker that if he or she will go through the superficial motions, incantations, and repetitions of praise and worship, the floodgates of provision will open.

I describe *delight* to our trainees in the mentoring seminars, reminding them of who the writer was, and then ask: "What would be *your* desires? What would *you* wish for had you been, as David, in the presence of the Father?" There is often an uneasy quietness; the students are reluctant to answer too quickly. Often it is a meek soul who ventures an answer: "I have been with my Father. My desire would be His desires for me. He is my desire." And so it is. Creator turns to creature and says: "Here is your purpose; here is your inheritance; live it out by my grace." This becomes more meaningful when we return to the larger context of Psalm 37 in chapter 4. There, we learn it is possible to prevent the desires of our hearts from ever occurring.

CHAPTER TWO

Mentoring from a Kingdom Perspective

MUCH OF THE DEBATE SURROUNDING CHURCH-BASED MENTORING REVOLVES AROUND THE QUESTION "FOR WHOM DO WE MENTOR?" WE MUST DISTINGUISH BETWEEN THE KINGDOM AND THE CHURCH TO further appreciate the emphasis put on *agape* in the previous chapter. *Agape*, like the *Shema* before it, drew us first to a singularity of focus on the Father, and second to an intensity of that focus. These were basic to the intimacy between mentorees who lived out their purposes and the God who bestowed those purposes.

The scholarly attention given in recent years to the systematic theology of the kingdom of God does not need further discussion here, other than to address the practical theology of mentoring from a kingdom perspective. For this I have ample reason. My radical approach to mentoring, by casting it in the context of *agape* and its four purpose-generating pillars, points in the direction Christian mentors are to follow. The kingdom, for all else that can be said about it, was a product of *agape*.

This chapter has three objectives. First, I define the kingdom of God. Second, I distinguish between the kingdom and the institutional church. Third, I develop how mentoring should occur in the light of these distinctions.

UNDERSTANDING THE KINGDOM

Hamid is a good friend of mine. He is an Iranian. I was told his native name means *praise*. When he was growing up, he

21

wanted to be an outstanding soldier. His family experienced torture by the Soviets who had crossed the border into northern Iran. As a youth, he saw his father cut in half with machine gun fire, and he saw his mother bludgeoned to death as she ran down the street trying to escape Russian soldiers. Hamid joined the military and eventually became deputy chief of staff of the air force under the Shah of Iran. He was the chief operations officer and the lead test pilot for the air force. He made frequent trips to the United States to test and approve planes for purchase by his government. In America, he met Suzzie whom he married and took back with him to Iran.

In the early days of our acquaintance, Hamid frequently, admiringly, and passionately talked about the Shah, always referring to him as King—"King this; King that; King said; I wanted to please King; I loved King; King was my life; I give my life for King." I was listening to more than a patriot. I was listening to a man obsessed with and possessed by the Shah of Iran—the king. What affection this was of a seasoned warrior for his commander in chief.

The Shah died in Egypt where he had received treatment for cancer. Then came the revolution. Hamid escaped to the United States in order to avoid the assassination ordered on all who had been close to the Shah. Short of escape, death was a certainty. We would meet at his place of business and talk late into the evening hours. The conversations were frequent, intense, and detailed, and they resulted in a kindly affection between us.

An intellectual transfer was necessary to move from Islam to Christianity. One night while continuing in my efforts to explain the gospel in a way it could be understood, it suddenly hit me; the gospel of Jesus is also the gospel of the kingdom. I blurted out, "Hamid, Shah is dead and Iran—his kingdom as you knew it—is no more; King Jesus and His unshakable kingdom are alive." Silence. Stunned silence.

Seconds clicked off one at a time, adding up to minutes, and each minute seemed an eternity. Thankfully, I had the presence of mind to honor this man's silence. Then a tear. Another. The truth of what I had said began to sink in, deeper and deeper into this utterly committed man's soul. First, there was an almost imperceptible shudder running the length of his disciplined and sinewy body (he had thrice been national weight lifting champion). He raised his head slowly, finally comprehending the truth of what had been said. Then he whispered with a calculated definitive resolve unparalleled by most of the confessions I had heard at many church altars over the years, "I follow King Jesus; His kingdom will be my kingdom." Hamid never turned back on that resolve. To relate all the events that have occurred in his life since then would occupy volumes among the annals of saints who with great suffering have proclaimed the gospel of the kingdom.

Westerners have only a half-hearted understanding of the idea of a kingdom. Oh, we are comfortable when referring to the *Wild Kingdom* television series, or the *Lion King* movie, or the king of the beasts. Animals have kingdoms, at least on television's Disney or Discovery Channels and in Hollywood. *Kingdom* does not arouse for Westerners the totality of power that resides in the hands of kings. We have difficulty envisioning absolute power. We are an arrogant, self-willed, and often anarchic people. Moreover, we are not helped much by the pomp and ceremony of the British monarchy which is probably the closest most of us have come to knowing about kings. We admire the royal family from afar but have little reverence or awe for or fear of it. For those who have tasted of the severe, total, arbitrary, and capricious power of contemporary Middle Eastern rulers, the story would be different. Yet, it is this kind of total power that resided in the biblical idea of kingdom.

We fail to comprehend the idea that a biblical kingdom comes closest to our idea of government. A proper understanding of Isaiah 9:6–7 would help, but it doesn't really affect most of us. It is only a part of Christmas pageantry in our churches, a reason why we are supposed to be happy in the midst of the holiday season. We fail to see Isaiah's prophecy as a victory song associated with battle and a vanquished enemy. There shall be a government with a ruler called Mighty God and Prince of Peace, and this absolute ruler's government shall just keep increasing to become total! We also miss the connotation in this context of the Bible's use of *peace*. Isaiah's Prince of Peace was Lord Jesus. He gave a face and a name to the idea of kingdom. He was king, master, ruler, owner, and sovereign lord all wrapped into one.

Hamid had captured these ideas. He knew about governments with absolute rulers; he knew about wars where there was only one victor. He knew what it meant to "sue for peace" and to "negotiate the terms of peace," where one government, such as Japan at the conclusion of World War II, capitulated and accepted the terms of peace handed over by General Douglas MacArthur on the deck of the battleship *Missouri*.

In our conversations, Hamid had heard ideas that provided him a new psychology, a new set of lenses, with which to see a reality involving Jesus Christ who was Hamid's new Significant Other. Much of what we had discussed now made sense. Seek first the government of God. My government is not of this world. The government is within you. The government has come and keeps on coming. We have an unshakable government. God transfers us from the government of Satan to the government of His Son. In the affairs of men, the government will rule. The deliverance of men from sickness and demons means the government has touched you. Go proclaim the government of God.

The government had a Prince of Peace. *Peace* is a warring term, as expressed above. The colloquial Greek word for peace, *eirene* (synonymous with the Old Testament *shalom*, as used in Isaiah 9:6–7), connoted an all-powerful magistrate whose beneficence gave villages tranquility and serenity. You could take a walk in the dark early morning hours to seek relief from the heat of the previous day and no one would mug you or break into your house. We can live with the kind of king who administers that kind of *eirene*. But that kind of peace comes with a price: living under the authority of the king—seeking, accepting, and appropriating his government.

Peace comes with a price: living under the authority of the king—seeking, accepting, and appropriating his government.

This all made sense to Hamid, and he made the transfer of allegiance. He became a Christian. In the place of King, Shah of Iran, Hamid became obsessed with and possessed by King Jesus and the kingdom of God.

Bible-oriented Christians seldom deny the concept or the reality of the kingdom. The biblical view of the world tells of two domains or kingdoms. The kingdom of God is the realm of God's authority and government. In this sense, the kingdom is the totality of persons submitted to the lordship of Jesus Christ. Everything about this kingdom is good. Satan rules the other domain and its varied forces of wickedness. Everything about this domain is evil.[1]

Important to our understanding is that the "kingdom has come," and "the kingdom is yet to come." In the first sense, the kingdom came into existence from Christ's first preaching and ever since people have been entering it (John 3:3; Matt. 21:31; Luke 17:20–21). We understand that this aspect of the kingdom will continue until there is a final harvest at the end of the age, the angels of God settle terminal issues, true believers are separated from the false, and Satan is defeated (Gen. 3:15; Matt. 25:1ff; 25:14ff). In the end, the kingdom will fully have come when the total rule of Christ prevails. Our description of the working of kingdom in the present day continues as we examine how it played out in Hamid's life.

Hamid's decisive shift of allegiance from one kingdom to another followed his saving faith in Jesus Christ (Col. 1:13). He recognized his sin, his need for salvation and redemption, his need to confess and seek forgiveness, and his need to commit to Jesus first as Savior and then to follow Him as Lord. He experienced the remarkable gift of *agape,* and, because his faith was a saving faith, he expressed his own love for God by obedience to His commandments (John 14:21). His habits changed. He began to run his business according to biblical principles, and the business flourished. (This is to say that it became a kingdom business.) He committed himself to daily reading and study of the Bible, and he became fluent, along with his boldness, in his ability to share his faith with others. (This is to say that he walked among people as a kingdom man.) He disciplined himself to pray in solitude three times a day. Thanksgiving, praise, and worship were a regular part of these times alone with God. Peace came to him, his wife, and their home. (The home became a kingdom home.) The kingdom prevailed in many areas of his life. He understood the kingdom was in his heart (Luke 17:21), and the kingdom exhibited itself wherever he went and in whatever he did (Matt. 6:10). There was no question in Hamid's mind that Lord Jesus Christ—name and face—was the embodiment of the kingdom (Matt. 1:23; 12:28). Hamid was an excellent disciple and mentoree.

During one particularly traumatic period, Hamid and Suzzie were falsely accused of a serious crime, and so dramatic was their public testimony before their accusers, before the magistrates in the courts, and among their attorneys, that people from many different churches in their community came to their support.

Their attorney said to me: "I have heard of the body of Christ and of the kingdom of God all my life in my church, but this is the first time I have actually seen them impact an entire community. The unity among the churches is remarkable!" Through the testimony of these two kingdom people, the kingdom swept through a community and made its mark.

CONTRASTING THE CHURCH AND KINGDOM

In recent years, my mentoring responsibilities have shifted from primarily a mentoring of individuals to more the conducting of training seminars and developing of mentoring programs. Early in the planning with the pastoral staff of a church-based program, it has been my practice to explain what my biblical position was on mentoring, which was that I trained God-called mentors who would assist God-called mentorees to realize, understand, and develop their God-given purposes. Our programs do not give preference one way or another to church- or parachurch-based purposes over those lived out in the secular marketplace. God calls people to a multitude of pursuits and equips them with grace to accomplish kingdom-oriented responsibilities. In these conferences with senior church staff, I reserved one question for the end, and it went something like this: "You have said you would like your members to mature and come into their calling and purposes in God, and this certainly is what I am dedicated to accomplishing. Now, I have a question. Let us suppose after we train a highly attractive and desirable young person whom you have been looking at to put into a junior staff position, that mentoree feels he or she is to leave the church and fulfill God's purposes at another church, in the secular marketplace, or in some distant community. Would you be willing to release that person even though you have made a substantial investment in them?"

This is a critical question, for it potentially pits the interests of the institutional church against the dictates of the King in behalf of the kingdom. Every pastor has many slots to fill as he seeks to manage his organization more efficiently and effectively. This is understandable and warranted when the purposes of God for the mentoree are matched to the church's needs. Unless one understands the difference between the kingdom and the institutional church, mentoring programs may provoke conflicts between program leaders and leaders of the larger organization. Nowhere in the Bible is the church presented as being the same as the kingdom. Jesus' central message was the kingdom (Matt. 10:7, 8). Only twice did He reference the church and then only in its institutional sense (Matt. 16:18; 18:17).

We understand the church, as the body of Christ, to be the redeemed of all time—some already having gone to heaven, those living now, and those not yet born.

We understand the church, as the body of Christ, to be the redeemed of all time—some already having gone to heaven, those living now, and those not yet born. The redeemed include all streams of Christian doctrine—Orthodox, Protestant, and Roman Catholic.

We understand the kingdom in the sense in which it changed Hamid's life and as it applies to all people who commit themselves to the authority of Jesus Christ as Lord. Nevertheless, I have discovered over time that I need to identify points of contrast between the kingdom and the institutional church and apply these where they are relevant to the mentoring program.

Points of Contrast

My interest is not academic. I explore differences between the kingdom and the institutional church and apply relevant points to the mentoring programs, ever mindful that the mentoring program is part of the institutional church. Mine is not to put the kingdom and church into a competitive relationship where mentor program coordinators, mentors, and mentorees have divided loyalties. I am a church person; I work in the institutional church; I recognize its role in carrying out kingdom purposes. I am not ignorant of times when the two do come into conflict with each other—the church may have interests that are not true to the kingdom. One of the most obvious of these was discussed in chapter 1. To whatever extent the church departs in doctrine and practice from an *agape* orientation, it is not a kingdom church. If *eros* and *nomos* rule, I conclude Jesus does not.

Not all differences between the kingdom and the institutional church are important for our purposes. Hence, the reader's favorite difference may not be included in my list.

The invisible and the visible kingdom

The kingdom is invisible in the sense that we enter it by faith in Jesus Christ and incorporate it into our thoughts and motives. Our behavioral obedience to the Bible witnesses Jesus' words that "the kingdom is within you."

The kingdom is visible in the sense that the church, as the Apostles' Creed puts it, is a visible entity. It is the instrument established by Jesus and used by God to carry out the purposes of the kingdom. Here, the church preaches the kingdom; it does not preach itself. Because there is no gospel of the church, the kingdom is integral to any proclamation of the gospel, meaning the gospel of the kingdom is the gospel in its totality.

The juncture of the visible kingdom and the invisible kingdom in the personal religious experience may cause problems for the mentor and the mentoree, and the mentor has a responsibility to make the distinction clear. In the best of all worlds, the mentoree joins a church and has leaders who reflect kingdom principles. In practice this does not always occur. Hamid, my Iranian brother, reported back after joining a local church (at my urging) that, even as a young Christian, he recognized inconsistencies between what the Bible taught and how the church was promoting itself.

Kingdom-church reciprocity

A reciprocal relationship exists between the kingdom and the church. As the church proclaims the kingdom, the church grows in size and purity; as the church grows in size and purity, the kingdom enjoys increased proclamation. The proclamation of the kingdom causes change in the sense that when the church responds obediently to its demands, it in turn receives blessings, rewards, and protection (Acts 17:7–8, 11–12).

A commitment to *agape* by mentors and mentorees, at the expense of *eros* and *nomos*, will invariably have a redemptive and restorative influence on any church. The best evidence of this comes from those we have trained, whose transformed lives become salt and yeast in their places of service in the church as well as in the secular marketplace.

Ever mindful that a kingdom and *agape*-oriented mentor or mentoree is an integral member of the institutional church, they as individuals can exert influence on a congregation that otherwise lacks in obedience to kingdom principles.

External and internal

The church fully represents the kingdom when it exhibits both internal (Luke 17:21) and external (Matt. 6:10) qualities. The church is out of balance when only one of these occurs. The internal focus leans towards pietism, fatalism, and passivity. This emphasis focuses on personal growth in a variety of forms—counseling, support groups, discipling, and mentoring as examples. The external focus is activistic, reaching out to the community in an equally large number of ways—evangelism, social services, efforts at unity among congregations, and impact on local social institutions as examples. Both external and internal qualities are required if the kingdom is appropriately to be represented.

Mentors are required to assess the balance of their churches in these internal and external aspects and advise mentorees to seek balance in their lives. Mentors will assign tasks that have the effect of giving balance where it may have been lacking in the mentoree's life.

Division of labor

The church has members who occupy many functional, administrative, and leadership positions—pastors, evangelists, apostles, prophets, teachers, elders, and deacons. These persons carry out the purposes of the church to build it up and contribute to the maturity of the members to do the thousands of tasks required to represent the kingdom and bring glory to God.

Only when leaders properly proclaim the kingdom, however, will a true spiritual priesthood be produced (Exod. 19:5–6; 1 Pet. 2:5, 9; Rev. 5:9–10; 20:6). Mentors are members of the spiritual priesthood. They recognize the diversity that exists among other mentors (as having the unique deposits of God in them), even though they have the same responsibility to mentor. They also recognize the diversity of God's purposes in terms of how they work with their mentorees. Mentors are in a unique position to "preach diversity" of purpose since they witness it among the many mentorees who come for mentoring.

Church as social organization

The church, in its corporate sense, is subject to many of the same economic, political, and social forces that control other organizations in the community. Regulatory agencies can influence for

good or ill the organizational structure of the church, its membership, and its potency. The kingdom, on the other hand, is invisible
and unshakable (Heb. 12:27–28). A kingdom-oriented mentoring
program can function in a positive way by mentoring men and
women to assume important positions in the church so that it
gains in vitality. Mentors also can do this despite outside forces
that may be to the contrary.

One of the more important functions of mentors is to help
reduce the incidence of envy and jealousy in the church by advocating the uniqueness of individual God-given calling and purpose.
My experience has proved many times over that when mentorees
truly recognize their calling in God they cease looking at someone
else's ministry and walk tall and confident in their own.

The kingdom and church in tension

A friend and I were having heated fellowship, discussing a
desire he had to start a new movement in the church he was
attending. Roger was a respected senior statesman among
church leaders, a mentor of mentors, and he had a prominent
national ministry. He had retired several years earlier from the
business he founded and was financially independent. Roger had
spent his entire life in the church. He was a man of the Word.
Our relationship was one of mutual mentoring. I would take him
on for a few weeks; he would return the favor.

The point Roger tried to make was that God had given him a
task to do, and he felt others were stonewalling him. The local
leadership would not budge. I was comfortable with Roger's logic
and the biblical basis he offered, and I agreed he seemed to have
heard from God. We were friends, but I still would not pick up an
offense for him and defend him at the expense of his church.

"Friend," I said, "it appears you just don't know the difference
between the kingdom of God and the church." Despite his life-
long dedication, he agreed he was not clear on the difference.
"Explain," he said. I recited several of the foregoing principles
and then asked: "Are you going to obey God or fight churchmen?"

He agreed and concluded: "It's more important for me to be
obedient to the Lord than to contend with others, even though
they may be leaders in the church. I'll be quiet where I am and
remain there but go someplace else to do what God has told me to
do." He was at peace with his decision then and continues to be

several years after our talk. A spin-off of Roger's decision was renewed confidence and commitment. He was following the King, and the opinions or resistance of men took a lower position in his view of things.

Only someone versed in the differences between the kingdom and the church can contribute to Roger's circumstances. There are several considerations in negotiating the conflicts between kingdom goals and church goals. Not the least of these I already mentioned—do not pick up an offense for the aggrieved party. Next is the matter of the other person's level of maturity; we are less likely to give credence to the appeal of a younger Christian as compared to someone like Roger. Can the mentor trust that reasons offered by the mentoree have benefited from the unity of Scripture? I long have advocated that the mentor be skilled in biblical interpretation. On one occasion, a church board member came up at the conclusion of the training session and said: "I am on the board of my church. There are many decisions that I have a hard time squaring with the Bible, and as you know, I have a fiscal responsibility for the church as a corporation. Can you teach me interpretation skills?"

Church: time- and space-bound

The church in its institutional sense is time- and space-bound. The kingdom is eternal, invisible, and unshakable. The kingdom is like the warp threads running the long way of a fabric—everlasting, linear, without end. It just keeps on coming. Like weft threads running at right angles across the warp, the church is finite and intersects at unique historical points in the unfolding of God's kingdom.

Each generation has its peculiar church-based challenges to which it responds as a part of the kingdom's unfolding purposes. Yesterday's challenges and accomplishments, while important from the standpoint of understanding church history and its lessons, are not necessarily relevant or productive for today's needs and challenges.

The church's responsibility, including the role of mentors and mentoring programs within it, is to be responsive to the present moves of God.

What a humbling thought this is, for it accentuates the spatial and temporal nature and limitations of the institutional church. One does not need, nor is it always advisable, to repeat even the best of the past. Each movement of God has been sufficient for the age in which He destined it. The church, as servant to the kingdom, is time and space bound; to be relevant it must be responsive to God's plan. The church's responsibility, including the role of mentors and mentoring programs within it, is to be responsive to the present moves of God.

Will biblical mentoring be relevant beyond this generation? At the last count, mentors have been on the scene to do God's will for over thirty-five hundred years. This is no blip in human history. Only the elder has enjoyed a similar record. It seems that the mentoring relationship is a foundational means God has used to accomplish His purposes.

The weft of the fabric, I have said, transects the linearity of the warp. In this sense weft, like the church, is time and space bound. History shows us, however, that at every point where weft and warp met, without regard to space and time, there were mentors providing for the stability and continuity of God's plan. The purposes to which God calls humankind may change relative to era and location. The guiding mechanism has not changed.

CHAPTER THREE

Biblical Principles of Mentoring

BIBLICAL PRINCIPLES OF MENTORING DERIVE FROM RECORDED
RELATIONSHIPS BETWEEN TEACHER AND STUDENT. WHILE NOT
EXHAUSTIVE, THE TEN PRINCIPLES SUMMARIZED HERE ARE
sufficient for most mentoring relationships. Scripture is generous
with examples like these, and if we infer correctly, the nature of
the relationships approximates what we call mentoring. We have
tested these principles in churches across America with people in
training as mentors. Serendipity, as she so often does, however,
has transformed many mentors-in-training, and pages of testimonies attest to the breadth of impact they have had.

THE PRINCIPLES AND RESPONSIBILITIES

The Gradual Nature of Spiritual Growth

The writers of Scripture used metaphors drawn from agriculture to express eternal truths. These communicated to
first-century listeners the ideas of planting and waiting for the
sprouts, blades, strong stalks, mature heads of grain, and then the
harvest (Mark 4:28–29; 1 Cor. 3:6–9). The seasons that traverse
twelve months do not bend to man's desire for fruit out of season.
This is as true today as it has been for all of history. David knew
fruitfulness was a function of "being in season" (Ps. 1:3b). The
farmer had to plan and follow basic principles that produced the

33

desired yield (Ps. 1:1–3a). Luke applied the metaphors of growth and maturation to social and spiritual growth. Be faithful first in small things, he wrote; then graduate to larger things. Be faithful in natural responsibilities, and God will give you spiritual responsibilities. Finally, be faithful as someone else's employee, and you will earn the right to be a business owner and entrepreneur (Luke 16:10–12). Preachers and teachers still use these illustrations, and generations of people wanting and waiting to mature physically, socially, and spiritually grasp the meanings. These all convey a sense of "process." Immature people in any area of learning have to yield to the process in order for it to work its intended purpose. The character quality required for this is patience.

Americans, however, are an impatient lot. Our culture conditions us to expect all things in the shortest time possible. Impatience is one of our gods—the god of the here and now. This has all but evaporated what social scientists refer to as delayed gratification, or the willingness to put off today so we can experience and better appreciate a sought-for goal sometime in the future. As the need for postponement has diminished, social scientists talk less of delayed gratification. Examples from modern life emphasize that waiting is less necessary. Primary among these is the plastic economy that encourages us to reward ourselves before earning what we spend. A close second are both modern telecommunications that transcend time and space at very little cost and technology that removes hours from making a cake from scratch by simply thawing it in a microwave oven.

Our conditioned expectations produce a predictable style of life, and, to the mentoree, this applies to matters of the mind and spirit.

How mentorees would like to discover their purposes in God on one day and live them out on the next!

Technology has changed man to the extent that technology, as earlier quoted from Peter Drucker, has become an extension of man. Will we ever be able to think of ourselves apart from our gadgets? "Psychological ecology" refers to how we perceive and act toward our physical environment. Neurophysiologists in recent years have even suggested that the connectors—synapses—between sending and receiving nerves in our brains become conditioned to "expect" that our "personal schedules" will act in a consistent way. We are careful not to take these analogies too far. "Living fast with little delay" or loss of delayed gratification are learned behaviors. Our conditioned expectations produce a predictable style of life, and, to the mentoree, this applies to matters of the mind and spirit.

Mentor's responsibility; mentoree's response

Mentors recognize that a modern lifestyle desires results in the least amount of time. In our programs, we require that mentorees choose and reach two to three goals within four to six months. Success in little things, frequently repeated, builds hope in the purposes God has chosen for the mentoree.

Obedience and Unfolding Spiritual Truth

United States federal government bureaucrats have a principle for some people known as the "need to know," while others are at the level where they have a "right to know." The latter group has no piece of information withheld from them.

Jesus changed how He referred to the Twelve. Near the end, he called them friends, not to distinguish them from being disciples but to distinguish them from slaves. The distinction was one of intimacy and trust. Slaves do not know what the master does. Friends earn the privilege of joining an inner circle of intimacy. The disciples had grown in their obedience to Jesus' instructions even though it was not always easy to do so. It was not always easy to learn this skill. Repeated obedience, however, is what leads to trust and intimacy and results in the greeting: "I have called you friends, for all things that I have heard from my Father I have made known to you" (John 15:14). Within the inner circle, the disciples could hear the Father's voice.

In time, intimate relationships follow successive instances of obedience: "He who has My commandments and keeps them, he it is who loves Me; and he who loves Me shall be loved by My Father, and I will love him, and will disclose Myself to Him" (John 14:21).[1]

Obedience to God's Word brings disclosure and revelation of Himself. Obedience is a key to opening a door through which we walk into the presence of the Father, and it removes scales from our eyes to see what we did not see before. Best of all, we see Him. More is revealed each time we are obedient. Obedience takes on the quality of what the behavioral scientists call "habit strength" (a term I develop in greater detail in chapters 5 and 6), meaning that obedience gains the strength of a habit. It gets easier each time we are obedient. Like a muscle, obedience grows with repeated exercise. Obedience becomes automatic and is the discipline that moves us from being a disciple under training to a mentoree in the process of maturing divine purpose.

Obedience is a key to opening a door through which we walk into the presence of the Father, and it removes scales from our eyes to see what we did not see before.

Obedience is to do the will of God. Two words meaning *will* help us to understand what happens in the lives of mentorees as they develop the habit strength of obedience. The first *will* pertains to the desires, wishes, and will of God as expressed in Matthew 6:10 or 18:14. The written Word of God is of this kind. The mentoree's studies expose him or her to many precepts and principles that require an obedient response. The mentor helps interpret the way in which obedience should occur. Mentoree gradually ascends the spiral of obedience, each time experiencing more of the Father's pleasure. The habit strength of obedience brings rewards—the disclosure of the Father Himself!

The second *will* refers to the purposes of God. It is a deliberate design; repeated obedience results in the Father saying: "Here is what I have for you personally." It is as if the purpose conferred on believers is a sign of God's trust in us. I believe the transitions that Luke described in his gospel (10:12–16, referenced above) imply the same kind of shift from obedience to privilege. Had David not complied to the precepts of Psalms 119, Paul could not have given testimony to the purposes of God for David as king (Acts 13:21–22, 36).

I once described this sequence to a group of mentors-in-training. Some had graduated from college and a few had graduate ministry degrees. I came to the point of the previous paragraph, and one young professional suddenly raised his arm and cried: "Stop! I have prayed long and hard to know God's purpose for my life, and it seemed I was talking to a closed door. Now I know the door to be opened is for me to go back and obey what the Bible has already told me to do. I know exactly what that is! He can't trust me with His purposes until I have shown faithfulness in obeying what is written."

Mentor's responsibility; mentoree's response

Mentors teach that in the early months of the mentoring relationship, mentorees develop the skill of obedience to the general will of God as a requirement for better understanding the more specific purposeful direction of God in their lives. The latter, mentors explain, is dependent on the former.

Cutting the Chains that Tie Us Down

The person embarking on a journey can ill afford an excess load. I recall my first wilderness backpack trip with my brother. We planned for the High Sierras of California, but I took too much. Much of it was unnecessary. The high country is a magnificent adventure; the beauty unparalleled; the thirteen-thousand-foot altitude breathtaking (literally); the campsite and smell of the hot pine fire welcomed. I thoroughly enjoyed myself. This was true only when my load was lessened to that of an experienced packer. On later excursions to the high country, my pack was considerably lighter.

In the earlier days of His ministry, Jesus invited others besides the Twelve to be His disciples. Some were unable to respond for a variety of reasons (Luke 14:25–35). There were those who thought His words were "too hard." Some had loyalties to friends, family, and tradition that controlled their ability to make decisions. To these Jesus said: "You cannot follow me." Still others gave priority to the pursuit of personal reputation, self-esteem, status, and socially acceptable identities. To these Jesus also said: "You cannot be my disciples." To still a third group that was over-committed to material things, acquisitions, and wealth, He said: "You cannot be my disciples."

Three times Jesus said "You cannot." These people had followed Jesus from place to place, sometimes to savor the exhilarating healing and deliverance services, to drink in the new and exciting teachings, or to fill themselves during the hillside picnics. They must have yearned to climb in the yoke with Him. With tears of consternation, they tried to arise and follow, but they could not. It was not a matter of permission on Jesus' part; He had invited them. It also was not a matter of their will. Two mentorees had started in my program; one a young man whose early relationship with his father was horrible. Until the mentor was able to lessen the impact of past influences on this person's life, he could not move on to develop his purposes in God. In addition, there was a beautiful young lady, another mentoree, whose drive for status and position was so great and disabling that all the mentor could do was love her and build relationship. Mentoring came later.

The 1996 Olympic track competitions captured my attention the first time I saw Michael Johnson win the 200- and 400-meter sprints. What an amazing physique, what intensity of resolve. These were his moments—crouched low, one foot in the block, the other placed forward, his eyes closed, visualizing the line that he would cross. Crowds were screaming even before the report of the pistol in anticipation of his victory. Years of practice and body conditioning had taken precedence over pleasures, all in favor of the prize set before him. My mind raced back to the Luke 14 passage. "My Lord," I thought. "He has the desire, the potential, the will, but what if he were chained to the block by one foot; he would be unable to run the race."

Only those who are able to arise and follow have the privilege of understanding what the Good News means.

Encumbered people, the apostle concludes, were like salt that had lost its flavor—good for the manure heap and not much more. Illicit affections and foreign gods had weakened their resolve. They later may have wondered where they would have arrived had they been able to follow Jesus. He would have taken them into the presence of the Father. Only those who are able to arise and follow have the privilege of understanding what the Good News means.

Mentor's responsibilities; mentoree's response

The mentor often discovers barriers to progress early in the mentoring relationship and discusses the importance of their removal. The mentor and mentoree agree on a schedule of tasks designed to remove the barriers. The mentor then decides if he or she will simultaneously assign other tasks more related to the mentoree's purposes in God.

Respect and Deference for Leaders

Ours is a society given over to the familiar. Familiarity goes hand in hand with the impatience I described earlier. Our democratic heritage explains some of this, although it was the Renaissance that originated the idea that every man is a king and the status of kings is equal that of the commoner. Familiarity has become a ploy associated with mass marketing and marketing's efforts to break down the social distance between sellers and buyers. Familiarity calls one by his or her first name with the hope of reducing sales resistance. It therefore is not surprising to see this carried over to our more traditionally formal relationships, such as: child and adult, doctor and patient, professor and student, pastor and parishioner, vender and customer, and, alas, mentor and mentoree. With the disappearance of social distance has gone the predictability of the roles people play. Should we be surprised at our feeling betrayed after purchasing a less-than-desirable item merely because we yielded to the excessively personal and friendly salesperson who called us by our first name although we'd never met before?

Much of the respect and deference described in Scripture derives from the cultural norms of the time. The absence of respect and deference in Western society, in contrast, is increasingly normative. In the German language, *sie* (the formal *you*) is used when addressing any person in authority, such as the mentor. The mentoree is *du* (the informal or more personal *you*, as when addressing a friend, child, or servant). Other languages have similar distinctions, and they function as indicators of social distance, whether familiar and personal, or formal and respectful. Another example further helps us to understand our American English. In German, *friend* refers to a very small and intimate circle of people, and *acquaintance* refers to everyone outside the intimate circle. The opposite is true here. Everyone is our friend, and we claim but few acquaintances. These distinctions have a bearing on the nature of the relationship between mentor and mentoree. The lives of Moses, Ruth, and Elisha clearly illustrate this principle.

Moses and Jethro

Moses' father-in-law Jethro, the priest of Midian, brought Moses' wife and two sons to the encampment of the Israelites at Mt. Horeb in the wilderness. Moses earlier had served Jethro for forty years, tending sheep, and the old priest no doubt had mentored Moses on many things, beginning with shepherding, a difficult task considering Moses' background in the comfort of Pharaoh's court.

During his stay at Horeb, Jethro observed Moses sitting in judgment of the people from sunrise to sunset and took it upon himself to counsel Moses on how to lessen his workload. Moses respected his father-in-law. He readily deferred to the elder's counsel, and he appointed representatives from all the tribes to assist in the judging of the people (Exod. 18). Although a father-in-law, Jethro nevertheless was a foreigner to the Israelites; yet, he was making recommendations to the leader of more than a million people. Moses did not balk. He did not chafe because a foreigner was suggesting how to judge and govern. There is no record that Moses' hair stood straight on the back of his neck nor evidence he resisted the very old man (after all, Moses had by this time passed his eightieth birthday) merely to defend his authority. Simply, Moses deferred, and the counsel proved correct.

Ruth and Naomi

The devotion of Ruth, the widowed Moabitess, to her mother-in-law, Naomi, is a beautiful story. The Book of Ruth has held audiences captive for several thousand years and is historically important for its contribution to the genealogy of King David and of Jesus. Ruth returns to Bethlehem with Naomi to whom she pledges her loyalty and commits to accept Naomi's people and God. The account is particularly important as an example of an older woman mentoring the younger on how to win a husband and prepare for marriage.

The customs Ruth followed were numerous and exacting. Naomi gave detailed instructions. Ruth was to glean in the corners of the fields. She was to find the portion belonging to Boaz. By staying alongside the young women, adventurous young men were less likely to take advantage of her. She could sleep at the feet of Boaz but had to leave before daybreak so as not to cause embarrassment. Finally, she had to wait for Boaz to bring a proposal for marriage before the elders in order to give another kinsman first rights at claiming Ruth. Detail after detail, and Ruth said to Naomi, "All that you say I will do" (Ruth 3:5). What an obedient follow-up this was to her earlier, "Where you go, I will go, and your people and your God will be my people and my God."

This was more than a classroom lecture where teacher taught pupil. This was a practicum dealing with important matters of marriage and family and destiny. Learning required doing. The doing required trust and a respectful deference to the wisdom of Naomi. What if Ruth had not respected and deferred to Naomi? Her name would not have gotten the Bible, and her place, as ancestor to David and Jesus, would have been lost.

Elijah and Elisha

Older and more seasoned prophets mentored each generation of succeeding prophets. Care and discipline were the heartbeats of the training. It was God, however, who chose them. No one by deciding or wishing it to be so can become a prophet. God calls many; He chooses only a few (Matt. 22:14). Once conscripted for training, however, the demands on the neophyte were arduous and, even then, did not guarantee success. Apart from the low success ratio, discipline and training were the requirements of a regimen that few today would want to take on if they knew the personal sacrifice required to "speak the word of the Lord."

John and Paula Sanford describe how the elder prophet took the younger and systematically humiliated him, "crushing and breaking his pride, defeating him and revealing his smallness and incapacity before God."[2] "And Jehosaphat said, 'Is there no prophet of the Lord here, through whom we may inquire of the Lord?' Then one of the king of Israel's servants answered, 'Elisha the son of Shaphat is here, who poured water on the hands of Elijah'" (2 Kings 3:11, KJV). Elisha poured water over the hands of Elijah? Just what kind of criterion was this in evaluating a prophet? In the day of Elijah, pouring water was menial, demeaning, humiliating women's work. The purpose was to expose every rotten core of the mentoree so that, just as Paul, the mentoree had no reason for confidence in the flesh (Phil. 3:4).

"Test after test was put upon the neophyte. The test was a success only if he failed to pass it."[3] No student could possibly have passed unless he or she had utmost respect and unquestioning deference for the mentor. The only test intended to be passed should now be evident—the prophet had to recognize the voice of the Lord and speak forth only His words.

The church can be a close fellowship among people who in time share many personal moments and know each other's anxieties and fears. From this fellowship come mentors and mentorees. The mentor may have known the mentoree for some time, and they are on a first-name basis. The social distance often necessary for respect and deference may not exist, thus putting both mentor and mentoree in positions where their informal roles conflict with the formal requirements of the mentoring situation. However the dilemma is resolved, the principle of respect and deference must remain as a basis for formally guiding mentorees in their purposes in God. An obvious evidence of deference in mentoring is the mentoree's unquestioning completion of assigned tasks and his or her accountability to the mentor.

Mentor responsibilities; mentoree response

Mentors are to tell mentorees the stories of Moses, Ruth, and Elisha, to illustrate the principle of respect and deference and how it was part of God's plan. Mentors, for the most part, like to be accepted, but the older mentor courts trouble when allowing someone fifteen to thirty years younger to address him or her in the familiar. Mentors will often make difficult demands on the mentorees, and mentorees will have greater difficulty accepting assignments from someone who is a "buddy."

Selective Recruitment

The most intensively mentored group of men were the twelve disciples who spent three years with Jesus. There were at first many, perhaps as many as five hundred, and these were narrowed to seventy, and then, as His ministry progressed, Jesus selected the Twelve. In a parenthetical sense, He called many, but He chose the Twelve for the specific purpose of accomplishing His long-term goals. Jesus' message was the kingdom; His method was evangelism; His strategy was to produce carefully selected and intensely trained men. Two principles are important for selective recruitment: the faithfulness of those who follow and the mentor's commitment to the mentoree.

Faithfulness

Faithfulness separates out some from the rest. Paul instructs Timothy to discriminate in choosing those who receive a higher privilege of service. A liberal paraphrase of 2 Timothy 2:2 illustrates this: "The things you have heard from me in the presence of many witnesses, I want you to teach [from our word *didactic*] the same message to others. Remain alert, and single out faithful men who, by virtue of having stuck with it, live out their lessons and demonstrate a higher quality of results in their lives. These are the ones who will end up teaching others."

What kind of people exhibit faithfulness? They are those who are loyal, reliable, dependable, and believable.

There will always be those we teach and who learn, are tested, and get straight A's on the exam. These are the didactic geniuses. The perfect recall of information, however, is not a criterion for faithfulness. Recall is a function of mental ability; faithfulness indicates character. Paul is stretching Timothy's perspective. He is pushing him past the days of the temple when youth sat at the feet of the priests and scribes and asked erudite questions.

Paul knew the wise farmer separates out the seed wheat from the wheat he converts to flour and grouts. The wise shepherd knows how to choose lambs that become the best breeding stock. Farmers and ranchers know how to separate out the best to reproduce clean lines of stock and bigger heads of grain, in order to perpetuate pure lines and strength of the species. These are principles that have far-reaching implications for the quality of leaders required by the body of Christ. Mentorees, like the highest quality seed wheat and breeding stock, reproduce pure offspring.

Commit a trust to others

Faithful men have committed or imparted the Word as a deposit or as a trust to protect. Timothy recognized the gravity of such a charge. Paul had used the same word in his first letter to him: "This charge I commit unto thee, son Timothy, according to the prophecies which went before on thee . . ." (1 Tim. 1:18, KJV). The same intensity with which Timothy received the prophetic word and charted his future, was the intensity with which he was to deposit the Word into faithful men. Peter uses the same word to describe suffering saints who were to commit the keeping of their souls to God in doing well, as unto a faithful Creator (1 Pet. 4:19).

Mentor's responsibility; mentoree's response

Selective recruitment occurs at two levels. First, those who nominate mentorees agree to do so using criteria provided by the program coordinator. Second, the program coordinator and mentor examine candidates in terms of their personal qualities during interviews and from questionnaires the candidates offer in evidence of past behavior.

Selective Attention

Americans value equality. History teaches we are born equal and thereafter become unequal. Nevertheless, "fairness" has entered public policy in an attempt to reduce or remove differences among people.[4] The Father is not willing that any should perish, but many do. He is willing that all grow to maturity, but not all do. The parables of the landowner who paid equal wages for unequal work and the unfaithful servant who failed to invest his master's money do not speak of equal chances or equal outcomes (Matt. 20:1–8; 25:15–20). Parables such as these concern advocates of fairness. Biblical stewardship over mentoring also assumes unequal outcomes. Some receive more opportunities than others do, and this certainly is the story of the Three.

To Peter, James, and John, Jesus variously gave the keys to the kingdom, invited them to the Mount of Transfiguration and later to the Garden of Gethsemane, assigned responsibility for care of His mother, included them when He healed Peter's mother-in-law, allowed one to show affection by resting his head on the Lord's chest, and revealed the apocalyptic vision. His inspiration led the Three to write letters and one gospel that later were included in the Canon. One letter—the Revelation—foretold the end of history and the commencement of Christians' rule of the universe alongside the Lord of the Universe. The other nine disciples had lesser responsibilities, details of which have been lost in the annals of church history or mentioned only as folk legend. Even among future mentorees or mentors, the leader singles out some for special attention, and these differ in how they are treated.

Mentor's responsibilities; mentoree's response

Mentors identify some mentorees for special attention, sometimes based on performance and sometimes based on God's revealed choice for greater responsibilities. The wise mentor tries to minimize any comparisons between mentorees that give rise to jealousy and envy. Mentorees therefore are encouraged to realize that purpose is an act of God and not man.

Proper Timing and Matching

One of the more intriguing stories of discipling, aborted relationship, and later mentoring and ministry occurs in the life of John Mark, the nephew of Barnabas. The story begins when Joseph, a Cyprian Levite (Acts 4:36) and landowner who, perhaps during Pentecost, was converted to Christianity, gave land as a gift to the apostles, and received from them the name of Barnabas, meaning "son of encouragement."

Following Paul's conversion and sojourn in the desert, Barnabas introduced Paul to the disciples at Jerusalem to attest to the legitimacy of Paul's conversion and to assure the elders that this rogue believer would cause no trouble (Acts 9:27). For a time Barnabas and Paul traveled together. We can imagine Barnabas mentored Paul, perhaps on the finer points of doctrine and certainly on how to behave in a civil manner in the presence of the early church, especially among new believers whose worldly accomplishments were more humble than Paul's.

Young John Mark came along as a helper on some of the missionary journeys, and during these times the apostolic team discipled him. This was quite an honor for a young man likely in his middle teens (Acts 12:25; 13:5). When the missionary team arrived at Pamphylia, John Mark left them and returned to Jerusalem (Acts 13:13). The Scripture does not reveal what the problem was, whether he was ill, homesick, or just wanting some of his mother Mary's home cooking (Acts 12:12).

Whatever Mark's problem, "Paul kept insisting that they should not take him along who had deserted them in Pamphylia and had not gone with them to the work. And there arose such a sharp disagreement that they separated from one another, and Barnabas took Mark with him and sailed to Cyprus" (Acts 15:36–39). The match between John Mark and Paul was not to be at this time.

Barnabas sided with John Mark. Speculation has it that Barnabas completed the young man's discipling and then mentored him to maturity and ministry. Evidence of John's maturation is seen sixteen years later when Paul requested Mark's return to the ministry. Mark eventually returned as a member in good standing of the team. The timing for John Mark's ministry was complete, and he later wrote what became the Canon's second gospel (2 Tim. 4:11; Col. 4:10).

Two principles emerge in the story of Paul and Mark. The first is that Paul obviously was not the right person to mentor the young man. The Lord, not man, places His sheep in flocks, and the Holy Spirit jointly fits each together in the body of Christ. There are mentors fully capable of mentoring a great diversity of mentorees. In the economy of God, nevertheless, we are constrained to seek the right match. We cannot be so impressed with the concept and process of mentoring that we make arbitrary connections of any mentor with any mentoree. For John Mark, it was Barnabas, and not Paul, who proved to be the right man to disciple and mentor him.

The second principle is that of timing. John Mark would have his day—a time and a place and the right person to be his mentor. Young men and women need to know about John Mark. Mentors need to assure a young person there will be a time when mentoring will occur and it will lead to the fulfillment of God's purposes.

Mentor responsibility; mentoree's response

Church leaders sometimes recommend candidates unacceptable for mentoring. An unacceptable candidate is one who has been insufficiently discipled, in that he or she lacks understanding of basic doctrine or exhibits immature behavioral or character qualities. The program coordinator or mentor explains that rejection of admission to the program can be a temporary thing. We tell the story of John Mark. When feasible, the mentor and failed candidate agree on a course of action that hopefully will result in later admission.

Availability, Accessibility, and Association

I have had numerous mentors—as a lad working on our family's ranch, later as a junior manager of an evangelistic youth organization, then when doing biophysics research at the university, and eventually when learning the skills of a college department chairman under the tutelage of a wise older scholar. Not one of these could have sufficed as a "mentor-for-life." After I became a professional in my field, one mentor stands out and exemplifies the principle of availability, accessibility, and association.

In the mid-1970s, I experienced spiritual changes that called for a "senior statesman" in my life. Pastor Lloyd Fuss was that man. I met him at a local conference and realized immediately he was the one I would ask to "shepherd" me. I do not hesitate in mentioning Lloyd's full name, for I want others to know the value I place on him and his role in my life during a critical period.

Lloyd had entered ministry later in life after a successful business career. He did not have graduate college degrees. He was pretty basic and reasonable in his logic; he had an iron-tight handshake; and most of all he loved the members of his small flock.

Lloyd was available. He preached on Sunday morning, held office hours, and taught on Wednesday evenings. I listened carefully to him; I admired how he led in worship. In these areas, however, he was seldom accessible. I could not tap him on the shoulder and ask a question during the sermon. I traveled in my work, and it was not easy to get an appointment because of his full schedule. He became accessible, though, when he invited me to call him any time I wanted, or to come over to the property where other church members were building a new church so that we could talk during lunch breaks. I liked that.

Often when I got up early, prepared a pot of coffee, and looked out the window, Lloyd would be sitting there in his car at five-thirty in the morning, not quite sun-up, waiting. There had been no phone call the evening before. "Do you want to bring your cup out to the car? How 'bout freshening mine? Are you free today so we can drive up to Pennsylvania and get supplies for the church? We need to talk about some things I think you're ready to hear, and we need quality time." Accessibility had graduated to association. Jesus took the disciples aside, alone, in a quiet and secret place. This was His method.

I never failed to learn from Lloyd during the times he was available or accessible. However, having captured the model of Jesus, Lloyd knew, as I do now, that availability and accessibility do not suffice for association. Association is the setting in which one person commits a spiritual trust into the account of another, to cherish and build on it and live out God's purposes in his or her life.

Any absence of spending quality time with people makes the development of building leaders an illusion, and mentors must have this burned into their minds. Robert Coleman comments on Jesus' association with the disciples: "After all, if Jesus, the Son of God, found it necessary to stay almost constantly with his few disciples for three years, and even one of them was lost, how can a church expect to do this job on an assembly line basis a few days out of the year? Whatever method of follow-up a church adopts, it must have as its basis a personal guardian concern for those entrusted to their care."[5]

Mentor's responsibility; mentoree's response

The greatest challenge to the mentor will be to set aside time to be with the mentoree. The greatest challenge of the mentoree will be to keep appointments. The mentoring relationship cannot become another didactic "teacher-student" relationship.

Demonstrating the Life

The Lord's example becomes our game plan (John 13:15; 1 Pet. 2:21). Paul repeated the principle in reference to himself as an apostle (2 Thess. 3:7, 9). There were basics Jesus demonstrated when discipling the Twelve, such as how to pray (Matt. 6:5–14); and He Himself never let up praying as a critical strategy in bringing the Divine into all the affairs of life. He taught them the importance of using Scripture by His frequent references to the prophets (Luke 4:14–20); and He never stopped doing this, even when on the road to Emmaus following the Resurrection (Luke 24:13–27).

Demonstration frequently will be spontaneous, so much so that the mentoree unexpectedly catches the mentor in the act as if it is the most natural thing in the world. The psychologist calls this "incidental learning." Jesus was spontaneous with the woman at the well, teaching her about true worship. He conducted a healing service in the middle of a lecture when a man was let down through the roof. He passed through a cemetery on the way to a meeting somewhere and took time to expel demons from a maniac. He was having a good time at a wedding feast and ended up producing vintage wine. He was lounging at a table for a meal, chatting with community leaders, and dared to allow a former prostitute to wash his feet with tears and expensive perfume. Time after time, it was spontaneous. The setting for the parables varied, but the method was spontaneity. Pulpits and lecterns work against spontaneity. The mentor has to be in the field of action in order to demonstrate life's lessons.

The mentor's life contains natural and spiritual deposits put there by God. The mentor is an exhibit before the mentoree, and the mentoree follows the mentor as he or she follows Christ (1 Cor. 11:1; Phil. 3:17f; 1 Thess. 2:7, 8; 2 Tim. 1:13; Phil. 4:9).

Mentor's responsibilities; mentoree's response
The mentor looks for occasions to demonstrate the practical skills for which he or she is formally mentoring another, while always having in the background the scriptural principles to embellish the natural. The mentoree is encouraged to observe the mentor and to ask questions of all he or she does.

Delegating Responsibility

Delegation signals a transfer of authority to the mentoree, requiring greater independence and less reliance on the mentor. The measure of a mentor's success is the duplication of himself or herself in the lives of others. "Greater things than these you will do." Eventually, others end up doing what mentors must at some point cease doing. This requires an unusual kind of humility.

The measure of a mentor's success is the duplication of himself or herself in the lives of others. "Greater things than these you will do."

Jesus, during the first eighteen months of His ministry, delegated responsibility to the disciples only occasionally and then primarily for simple tasks and baptizing some people (John 4:2). At the beginning of his third tour of Galilee, well into the second half of His ministry, the disciples prepared for more involvement in the ministry. They were to go to the house of Israel first, to preach the kingdom of God, heal the sick, cleanse lepers, cast out demons, and raise the dead (Mark 6:7; Matt. 10:5; Luke 9:1–2; Matt. 10:8).

During these journeys, the disciples learned some difficult lessons, ones which inexperienced people or others not under the guidance of the mentor would have found difficult. Challenges awaited the disciples at every turn. Had they not been ready, Jesus would not have sent them out. His promises were not encouraging. They would be whipped and interrogated (Matt. 10:17–18). Men would hate them (Matt. 10:22–23). They were like sheep in the midst of wolves (Matt. 10:16). Retreat was not an option; the kingdom had come and responsibility for it was on their shoulders. Their failure to carry their own crosses relegated them to unworthiness in the kingdom (Matt. 10:34–38). The principle is clear: Mentorees who are sent forth in the way Jesus sent the disciples require mentors who are as seasoned as Marine drill sergeants or police SWAT or Navy SEAL team members.

The principle states the mentor must have had sufficient experience to not be surprised at what he or she sees, hears, or smells, and the mentoree must be conditioned to these as well. We quote often the question asked of the Swiss psychoanalyst Carl Jung by one of his mentorees, a future psychoanalyst: "Aren't you disappointed with man considering all the sordid things you know about them?" To which Jung was reported to have replied, "No, I am not disappointed, for I am not disillusioned." Jesus did not give up on those He was sent to redeem. Had He been disappointed He possibly could have. He knew His ministry was to a sinful crowd; He knew the hearts of all men; and yet He was not disillusioned about who and what they were. He did not expect them to act any differently than they did. He knew the Cross would solve whatever problems their human devices found impossible.

Mentor's responsibility; mentoree's response

The ultimate responsibility of mentors is to work themselves out of their jobs by delegating responsibilities to their mentorees. In accepting these, mentorees will inherit the unique purposes reserved for them by the Father and thereby perpetuate the unfolding course of the kingdom.

CHAPTER FOUR

Calling, Purpose, and Destiny

I WILL EXPLORE THE CONCEPTS OF CALLING, PURPOSE, GIFTS, AND INHERITANCE. I ALSO WILL COMPARE GENERAL INHERITANCE AND SPECIFIC INHERITANCE. THE FORMER IS AVAILABLE TO ALL WHO ARE IN Christ, while the latter seems to be reserved for those who meet conditions of readiness.

Mentorees' sense of calling and purpose is the major criterion for participating in our program. They know there is some kind of "fit" for them in the kingdom, and they look forward to a mentoring relationship in order to give substance to their inclinations. These are not just any mentorees, but those who have shown they understand basic doctrines of the faith, make an effort to act rightly, and have begun a lifestyle of character development.

Calling and a sense of purpose are personal, often vaguely defined impressions. They are more of an urge than an audible calling to something specific. I wish church leaders more often saw the "urge" in this way. Too often an expression such as "I think God is calling me or telling me to do something," is misinterpreted. Leaders quick to fill a vacancy will assign responsibility (any will do) to a person for some part of the church's program. When that fails to satisfy the person, additional assignments are given with the prospect that busyness is the more appropriate solution to someone's search for meaning. Another response of some leaders follows the Christian's expressed interest in "things spiritual." Often tantamount to this interest is the suggestion that seminary training is somewhere

51

down the road. The obvious assumption here is that spiritual awakening comes only to future seminarians. We leaders have to slow down and explore carefully the latent desires of those in our care. I conclude this chapter with a checklist of how to determine calling and purpose in someone's life.

The awakening to purpose may lead to a place of service in the local church, in the sense that the church provides a place for growth and some initial form of service. Paul prayed that all believers would discover a piece of Jesus as his or her own personal inheritance (Eph. 1:18). Therefore, the pursuit and development of calling and purpose are among the more important challenges both mentor and mentoree have. Before we can handle them in an intelligent manner, however, we have to examine the way Scripture deals with them. Otherwise, we may commit the common mistake of misusing them.

THE MARKETING OF SUCCESS

Let's begin by dismissing counterfeit approaches. Success, purpose, calling, destiny, self-realization, and self-fulfillment— these, in the extreme, represent a Western world gone insane with *eros*! The urgency to find answers, solve problems, and attach oneself to the right political or religious leader, therapist, or entrepreneur is so great that it provides a ready-made demand for services by any individual or group willing to provide them. In all honesty, ours is not to peddle success, calling, or purpose, for these are in the purview of God and are His alone to provide. Ours is to cooperate with Him in bringing His children to maturity and productivity in the way He has determined. (The Mentor's Prayer in chapter 9 is an apt expression of this.)

The preoccupation with self and self-esteem has become the grist of a gigantic marketing empire, secular and religious alike.

The preoccupation with self and self-esteem has become the grist of a gigantic marketing empire, secular and religious alike. The success of marketers to make people feel dissatisfied with their own progress is nothing less than a secular miracle. The ability to create comparisons among audiences and incite envy by the have-nots has become a well-honed art.

Many religious organizations have kept up with this approach to success. Since the 1960s, thousands of religious publications have filled bookstores and racks in church lobbies. Many assure Christians their place in the sun of God's privilege, promise, potential, and performance. If I were not once a part of this spirit of the age and had not at one time watered down my own Christian faith by misuse of my professional background as a counseling, research, and consulting behavioral scientist, I would not be so free in writing as I am. That was then, and today is now!

This chapter has merit only because it recognizes that God's conferred value borne of *agape* constitutes the basis for calling and purpose and defines how we fellowship with Him.

CALLING AND PURPOSE

The Scriptures leave little doubt about God's initiative to call people with gifts and talents to carry out His purposes.

Gifts and the Call to God's Purpose

Scripture is rich with examples in which people's gifts and talents have led to the fulfillment of kingdom purposes, three examples of which I summarize here.

The tabernacle in the wilderness

In addition to the architectural details given for the construction of Solomon's residence and the temple, the most exacting recorded details we have are on the construction of the tabernacle in the wilderness. Exodus 35–39 provide detail after precise detail for the construction of the ark of the covenant, the tabernacle, and the priests' clothing.

> Then Moses said to the sons of Israel, "See, the Lord has called by name Bezalel the son of Uri, the son of Hur, of the tribe of Judah. And He has filled him with the Spirit of God, in wisdom, in understanding and in knowledge and in all craftsmanship; to make designs for working in gold and in silver and in bronze, and in the cutting of the stones for settings, and in the carving

of wood, so as to perform in every inventive work. He also has put in his heart to teach, both he and Oholiab, the son of Ahisamach, of the tribe of Dan. He has filled them with skill to perform every work of an engraver, of a designer, and of an embroiderer, in blue and in purple and in scarlet material, and in fine linen, and of a weaver, as performers of every work and makers of designs. Now Bezalel and Oholiab and every skillful person in whom the Lord has put skill and understanding to know how to perform all the work in the construction of the sanctuary, shall perform in accordance with all that the Lord has commanded." Then Moses called Bezalel and Oholiab and every skillful person in whom the Lord had put skill, every one, whose heart stirred him, to come to the work to perform it. (Exod. 35:30–36:2)

Many people have gifts and talents other than the ones described here. God's purposes for them may be to provide for their families and to carry out tasks that never come to public attention. In such instances, Christians do what they do well and as unto the Lord but without notoriety. Here, though, Bezalel is used, and the question begs asking: When were his talents developed? Was it in the wilderness or in Egypt? A lifetime of deposit had been invested in Bezalel while he was yet a slave; there was, after all, no reason or occasion to acquire and hone his many skills while wandering across desert wastes. Herein lies a principle. The purposes of God are like a large net, thrown out over the vast family of humanity whose bents, leanings, and talents have been acquired over a lifetime. The Father will choose at one point in the intersection of warp and weft of kingdom and church those uniquely prepared to fulfill His sovereign will for the moment.

The temple during Solomon's reign
The Lord provided Hiram from Tyre to oversee the building of the temple under Solomon. This fulfilled David's promise to Solomon that men with the necessary skills would come and build the temple (1 Chron. 28:21; 1 Kings 7:13–14). The artisans from Tyre lived during David's time. They developed their skills long before Solomon. However, their recruitment did not take place until the time of Solomon's rule.

Rebuilding the Jerusalem wall

The Book of Nehemiah describes a pagan king's cupbearer by the name of Nehemiah who had the skills of construction project and materials manager, negotiator, governor and public administrator, military strategist, and religious leader. These were not evident during his time in captivity as cupbearer, nor were they necessary. Nehemiah asked Cyrus, king of Persia, for permission to return to Jerusalem and rebuild the wall, which he did, but again one must ask: When were these management skills developed? They were learned no doubt before the exile, but were not commissioned by God until the fullness of time.

God Reveals Purpose

Scripture testifies that in Christ, God hides all wisdom and knowledge (Isa. 11:2; Rom. 11:33–36; Col. 2:3). He instructs the farmer how to perform his tasks (Isa. 28:26). Solomon derived wisdom and much knowledge from God who gave instructions to the farmer on how to assure the growth of crops (Eccles. 11:1–6).

God ordained the specifics and anointed Jesus' ministry in detail (Isa. 61:1–3; Luke 4:18–20); He provides gifts to everyone individually as He wills (1 Cor. 12:4–10, 28–30); and He chose David to shepherd Israel with the integrity of his heart and to guide the nation with skillful hands (Ps. 78:72). The sons of Reuben, Gad, and Manasseh were skillful in war (1 Chron. 5:18), and Chenaniah was skilled in music (1 Chron. 15:22). God gave knowledge and intelligence in every branch of literature and wisdom to the four Jewish boys held captive in Babylon. To Daniel He added understanding of all kinds of visions and dreams as well as special insight from the angel (Dan. 1:4, 17; 9:22).

Every good thing bestowed and every perfect gift from above is of God. They are evidence of the value conferred upon us as an expression of *agape* (James 1:17–18). The human family is incapable of sensing all that God holds in reserve for it (1 Cor. 2:9). We cannot hear nor perceive how God acts in our behalf when we tenaciously bind ourselves to Him (Isa. 64:4), or how He stores riches for those who fear and take refuge in Him (Ps. 31:19).

There are few better examples of conferred purpose than Jehovah's personal announcement to Israel near the end of their seventy years of exile in Babylon (Jer. 29:10–14).

"When seventy years have been completed for Babylon, I will
visit you and fulfill My good word to you, to bring you back to
this place. For I know the plans that I have for you," declares
the Lord, "plans for welfare and not calamity to give you a
future and a hope. Then you will call upon Me and come and
pray to Me, and I will listen to you. And you will seek Me and
find Me, when you search for me with all your heart. And I will
be found by you," declares the Lord, "and I will restore your
fortunes and gather you from all the nations and from all the
places where I have driven you," declares the Lord, "and I will
bring you back to the place from where I sent you into exile."

Dr. Edmund Sinnott, eminent biologist and dean of Yale
University's graduate school, years ago expressed a similar idea
in his own (then-unpopular) effort to reconcile between matter
and spirit.[1] His general thesis, woven throughout his book,
Biology of the Spirit, proposed that all the natural world moves
purposefully toward some goal; purpose never is in question; and
it is everywhere and in all places. However,
purpose is a philosophical, not a naturalistic
phenomenon. Hence, Dr. Sinnott wrote, only a
"purpose giver" will provide purpose.

*Purpose never is in
question, and it is
everywhere and in
all places.*

Oliver Wendell Holmes's quip that "most
people go to their graves with their best song still
in them" acknowledged the universality of "having
a song" but bemoaned the dilemma: "How does
one get his or her best music out where others can hear it?"

Dr. Laura Schlessinger, conservative talk show provocateur
with a weekly audience of twenty million listeners, contributes
her own idea of purpose. One day she was watching a docu-
mentary about the Holocaust with her son, Deryk. They
showed naked mothers and children lined up and executed by
soldiers. "When [Deryk] asked me who these people were, I heard
myself blurt out, 'those are our people,' and began to think of
myself as a Jew," says Schlessinger. She dove into Jewish texts
with the same intensity as she does everything else. One day,
reading in Genesis about the covenant between God and Israel,
she says, something clicked, and her life's purpose became
clear. "I ran downstairs and yelled [to my husband], 'Lew, I'm
a priest and my mission is to help God perfect the world!'"[2]

Dr. Schlessinger's skills existed long before her moment of insight while watching the Holocaust film. The horrific scenes awakened and gave those skills a focus they did not earlier have. She merely needed that "moment of discovery" for the commissioning to take place.

Christian businessman John D. Beckett is president of R. W. Beckett Corporation, headquartered in Elyria, Ohio. Beckett's father founded the company twenty-five years ago, and it now has a growing position of market leadership in the American heating industry. In an interview with Intercessors for America, Beckett described how, when he was a youth, he planned to become an Episcopal minister. His heart, nevertheless, was in engineering and business. "When I was accepted to MIT . . . I wanted to do cartwheels. But during college, and later in my business career, the nagging question recurred—was I in the highest calling—was I where God wanted me?"[3]

Beckett had no deficiency in engineering talent or business acumen. However, the question of purpose, calling, and destiny nagged at him. He tells how a step of faith resolved the question. "I completely relinquished my work and the family business to the Lord. I said, 'This business can't be Yours and mine at the same time.' Almost immediately . . . I believe He affirmed . . . I was exactly where He wanted me, that I was called to business. The New Testament tells . . . that everything is holy if . . . surrendered to and in harmony with the Lord. This includes our vocations as long as they are not contrary to His righteous standards."

The late–nineteenth century pastor and writer Charles Henry Mackintosh produced outstanding insights on the Scriptures. Widely read, *The Mackintosh Treasury* addresses our topic in the chapter on "Diversity and Unity":

> We see . . . in both the Gospels and in the Epistles . . . [how each] of the four Evangelists, under the guidance and power of the Holy Ghost, gives a distinct view of Christ. . . . Each one has his own specific line . . . but all agree. . . . So it is in the Epistles. . . . No two are alike, but all agree. There is no collision, because, like the four Evangelists, each moves in his own appointed orbit, and all revolve round the one common center. . . . Nor is it otherwise now in the Church of God. There are varied kinds of workmen, and varied lines of truth; and it is our

happy privilege, not to say our holy duty, to recognize and rejoice in them all. . . . We need them all, and therefore God has given them all.[4]

Mackintosh recognized that the diversity of gifts, parceled out in an apparently discriminatory way by a sovereign God, could lead to attitudes of uniqueness and, in turn, to the exclusion of others, unless we focus on Him who is our center.

Three Principles

Three valuable principles for the mentor emerge from these illustrations. First, purpose may be for a particular time in history, as seen in the biblical accounts of Bezalel, the architects and builders of the temple, the reconstruction of the Jerusalem wall, or the wisdom and prophesies of the Jewish lads in captivity. This is consistent with the emphasis in chapter 2 on the strategic God-ordained intersection of time- and space-bound purposes of the church with the unfolding events of the kingdom. The sensitive mentor encourages the mentoree to continue developing his or her skills, even though their eventual use is outside of present knowledge.

The second principle is a variation on the time-bound nature of purpose and its tie to periods in someone's life. Examples come from the lives of David (shepherd, poet, musician, warrior, and king), Joseph (court officer and public works administrator), Moses (shepherd, prophet, and leader), and Samuel (prophet, judge, and founder of the school of the prophets). All exercised roles vital to the Bible account. Many people today also will attest to progressive movements from one purpose to another; yet, as illustrated above, moderns such as John Beckett and Dr. Laura Schlessinger seem to have one primary place in God's economy.

The value of this for the mentor, and certainly for the mentoree, is that the mentoree's purpose may be one or several. In modern Western societies, as it most certainly is in America, a person in the secular marketplace may go through seven major job shifts in his or her work life. Our program has mentored people ranging in age from their mid-twenties to their mid-sixties, always with the assurance that God wastes no one's experience.

A familiar precept tied to our topic is relevant here. The mentor fosters God's *anointing* of the mentoree sometimes long before God *commissions* the mentoree to service.

The third principle is that God is a wise administrator, and all of us have a time and a place. I have known mentorees who would not accept counsel in line with this principle and rushed to carve out a path of their own making. Mentors need be sensitive to the possibility that some of their mentorees are of the "age of impatience" and refuse to remain in mentoring long enough to see God's fruit come to ripeness in God's time.

--- **THE NATURE OF INHERITANCE**

All who put faith in Christ are born into the family of God with all the privileges—general inheritance—associated with that birthright. For each of these there is also reserved a specific inheritance, or purpose, which is an integral part of "living in the kingdom of God."

The first three chapters of the letter to the Ephesians make frequent reference to our general inheritance in Christ. In Christ we are blessed (1:3); in Christ, we are the first to hope (1:12); In Christ, we are shown kindness (2:7); and in Christ, we are forgiven (4:32). These affirm the inheritance to all believers. These are our "family" rights and come to all who put faith in Christ.

General and Specific Inheritance: The Prodigal Son

The thought of an inheritance, and particularly its misuse, recalls the story of the profligate prodigal who prematurely asked his father for his portion of the old man's estate. The youth wanted to travel to a faraway land, find his fortune, and do his own thing (Luke 15:11–32). The story is a staple in church circles, and it has stirred many hearts.[5]

The younger son insists on his portion of the inheritance. The father gives in and parcels out the portion reserved for him. The son leaves; we are not told for how long but just that he goes to a faraway land. The father is in pain, and we imagine him frequently cupping his hands to his squinting eyes, looking into the distance, anxious for the son's return. He is not disappointed. The son returns, humbles himself before the old man, and, exposed for what he is, asks for a place among the father's slaves. Rather than punishment and an assignment to demeaning position, the father responds with mercy, forgiveness, and generosity.

The prodigal personifies *eros* and the drive for self-gratification. The older brother, as the story unfolds, personifies *nomos* as shown in his search for approval based on having lived, at least the way he sees it, a righteous life. The father is the exemplary model of the Heavenly Father who is the source of *agape*. There hardly has been a more stirring story of conferred value—unmotivated and spontaneous—upon an unrighteous person than when the father places the robe and ring on the wayward son. He reconfirms his son's place in the family, treats him as a royal visitor from afar, extends the right hand of fellowship, and invites the entire village to celebrate with him.

The issue is the manner in which the son handles his inheritance. Despite his debauchery, the profligate does not lose his position as a son. During his absence, he squandered a precious possession. Two elements are working here. First is the continuation of the son's relationship to the father and within the family, in their general sense, and secondly the son's misuse of his specific inheritance, of which we hear no more.

In the latter half of Ephesians, Paul refers to "in the Lord" and connects the phrase to behavioral prescriptions: walk worthy (4:1, 17), do not get drunk, be filled with the Spirit (5:17–18), obey parents (6:1), and be strong in the Lord (6:10). These phrases describe people who are obedient to the King; they live in accordance with the kingdom or government of God, as I described in chapter 2.

There remains the possibility that, like the prodigal, we refuse to live in a manner required for membership in the government of God. What happens then? Three passages—1 Corinthians 6:9–10, Galatians 5:21, and Ephesians 5:4—summarize the consequences of more than two dozen wrong behaviors, stating that those who practice these have no inheritance in the kingdom of Christ. Examples from the list are idolatry, adultery, swindling, angry outbursts, envy, jealousy, and coarse jesting.

Paul, as in all his letters, is writing to Christians, born again members of the heavenly family, saved, redeemed "in Christ"

Christians. Yet he makes a distinction between those who walk "in the Lord" and those who do not. Those who are "in Christ" and do not walk "in the Lord," receive a warning: You will lose your place in the kingdom if you practice wrong behavior. The emphasis is on the word "practice," as opposed to careless indiscriminate indiscretions (of which we are all occasionally guilty).

Many entrusted with the purposes of God have strayed from righteous behavior, losing the anointing for ministry and often the ministries as well.

We are familiar with children gathering at the bedside of the dying father, or in the office of the attorney to receive word on the disposition of the deceased father's estate. As children, all have a legal right to inheritance in the general sense of the term. Each individual child, on the other hand, inherits a specific portion more as a privilege and as the result of the father's discretion. The moments waiting for the reading of the will are fraught with anxiety: "Will I receive anything? What will it be? Will it be to my liking? Will it be what I deserve (or despite what I deserve)?" The same questions plague every child of God who in this life seriously tries to please the Father. *"Does my place in the family of God translate into a higher calling with purpose? Have I pleased my Father?"*

Many entrusted with the purposes of God have strayed from righteous behavior, losing the anointing for ministry and often the ministries as well. Their place in the family has not been lost, but they have forfeited (because of their disobedience) their place in the kingdom and the calling and purpose attached to it.

The mentor reminds the mentoree frequently that persistent obedience to the general wishes, will, and desires of God leads up to God's disclosure and release of His purposeful will for them.

Old Testament Inheritance and Possession of the Land

"Land" plays an important role in our analysis, for in earlier times it was the most common form of one's inheritable property or possession (Zech. 2:12). The land would give forth its fruit to those who remained obedient to God (Gen. 2:6), but as man mishandled his *inheritance of land*, the land became less fruitful (Gen. 4:12, 14). Land, as inheritance, represented a special relationship between

man and God, in the sense that the land was committed to man as
a trust for keeping (Gen. 28:14–15), but the fruitfulness of the
land depended on the obedience of God's people (Deut. 11:17).
Land is a metaphor for our specific inheritance in Christ; what
was said of land applies to our inheritance or purpose. Land
deserves a prominent place in any discussion of a person's
purpose in life. Those in ministry can learn much about God's
demands for the stewardship of their anointed gifts by giving
close attention to the principles associated with caring for the
land. Our mentors are most careful to communicate these principles to the mentorees.

The verb "to inherit, get possession of, or take as a possession" is used 60 times in the Hebrew Old Testament and the
noun—"possession, property, inheritance"—is used 220 times,
primarily in the Pentateuch and Joshua. Joshua entered and
captured Canaan. At first, it was only a possession because it was
not, in the usual sense of the word, an inheritance before the
time of occupation. Once occupied by all of Israel, the Promised
Land was distributed by leaders in order for it to become an
inheritance to individual tribes under Joshua's leadership. A
possession, once acquired, was potential inheritance to one's
descendants (Exod. 6:8; Num. 24:18; Deut. 2:5, 9; 33:4).

The Hebrew word *lot*, in its extended sense, represents a
particular possession (Josh. 15:1) as well as a "fate" or "destiny,"
which we often associate with purpose (Isa. 17:14). God controls
all things absolutely, so the result of casting a lot is divinely
controlled: "The lot is cast into the lap; but the whole disposing
thereof is of the Lord" (Prov. 16:33). In this sense, a *lot* is similar
to the specific aspect of a general inheritance, and beautiful are
Scripture's illustrations of this.

Caleb

Caleb, the faithful Israelite who refused to spread fear among
the people, received a special portion of Israel's general inheritance of the Promised Land. Forty years before, he and Joshua
brought back a good report of what the twelve spies had seen.
Caleb had seen a choice piece of hill country, today known as
Hebron, that he wanted for himself and his family. Because he
would not support the fear that overcame ten of the spies when
they saw the giants and because he held fast to God's promises,

God granted his wish when he returned to Canaan (Josh. 14:6–15). Caleb is the type of person Paul told Timothy to watch for and to place in ministry leadership—those who were faithful (2 Tim. 2:2).

Naboth

Responsibility for one's inheritance is a serious matter. This is seen in Naboth's remark to Ahab, the king: ". . . The Lord forbid it me, that I should give the inheritance of my fathers unto thee" (1 Kings 21:3 KJV). Unlike the prodigal in Luke 15 who squandered his inheritance, Naboth would not relinquish his inheritance to an undeserving person, though he was a king.

David

David recognized his particular callings in life. He had been prepared for each one. Looking at the green grass in someone else's pasture (i.e., someone else's calling and purpose in life) was not for him, for to do this would have been arrogant and presumptuous. Jealousy and envy were not his style either. I appreciate the humility with which he cried: "Oh Lord, my heart is not proud, nor my eyes haughty; nor do I involve myself in great matters [other than what you parceled out to me], or in things too difficult for me [which are outside your grace]. Surely I have composed and quieted my soul . . ." (Ps. 131:1–2a).

Possession and Dispossession Results in Inheritance

Israel's possession of the Promised Land introduces another element to our understanding of inheritance. A rendition of the word *possess* implies a corresponding *dispossession* of some earlier inhabitant. It is a warring term. Hence, Israel had to aggressively dispossess prior inhabitants in order to come into full possession of the land. I exercise caution here and try not to stretch metaphors beyond their allowed use. Nevertheless, the couplet "dispossess/possess" suggests that even as Israel's mandate was to completely dispossess the Promised Land of its enemies (with whom it eventually committed idolatry as a national sin), mentorees also must first dispossess themselves of *eros* and *nomos* in order to receive the purpose borne of *agape*. (The observant reader recognizes, I hope, that I am not suggesting here a right-eousness by merit, through which we gain membership in the family of God. That membership is by birth. Rather, obedience is the proof that a faithful family member is eligible to receive the promise of personalized purpose designed to carry out the larger purposes of the kingdom.) The Thirty-seventh Psalm lends credence to the dispossess/possess couplet.

Psalm 37

Psalm 37, in five passages, identifies the requisite qualities for inheriting the land as well as the qualities that prevent entry into it (verses 8–9, 10–11, 21–22, 28–29, and 34). Inheritance (or receiving purpose) depends on being humble, gracious, giving, righteous, and obedient to God's way. Disinheritance (or denial of purpose) results from fretting, doing evil, committing wicked schemes, borrowing and not repaying, being cursed by God, being the descendants of evildoers, and spying on the righteous. In the final analysis, Israel's possibilities depended on two things: responsible stewardship over the land and faithful obedience to the terms of the Covenant.[6]

The mentor cautions the mentoree: Guard your calling and purpose in God. Consider them as precious possessions.

The mentor cautions the mentoree: Guard your calling and purpose in God. Consider them as precious possessions. The price of fruitfulness and productivity is vigilance and obedience.

Inheritance and Calling in the New Testament

Jesus stands at the interface of the Old and New Testaments, for He is our inheritance. Jesus (Yeshua) represents all of the metaphors of the Old Testament. He is Moses, the King, Prophet, Rock, Temple. He also is our "inheritance." "In the New Testament the idea of inheriting [as a verb] broadens out to include all spiritual good provided through and in Christ, and particularly all that is contained in the hope grounded on the promises of God."[7] By virtue of being sons and daughters of God, we inherit a birthright (Gal. 4:30; Heb. 1:4; 12:17) and a gift is granted, to be distinguished from receiving a reward for keeping a law (Heb. 1:14; 6:12). We inherit on the condition of obedience to certain precepts (1 Pet. 3:9) and of faithfulness to God amidst opposition (Rev. 21:7).

The Bible's use of "calling" in the New Testament contains five instances of God's determining direction in our lives. They are as follows:

- The call to salvation which He most obviously cannot retract, and in which we have hope (Rom. 11:29; 1 Cor. 1:26; 7:20);
- The calling of specific peoples (2 Thess. 1:11; 2 Pet. 1:10);
- The calling to vocation (Eph. 4:1);
- The high calling, such as the service into which Paul had entered (Phil. 3:14); and
- The holy and heavenly calling, according to God's purpose (2 Tim. 1:9; Heb. 3:1).

Once called, God bestows gifts that are the content of purpose. Several examples illustrate this.

- All good and perfect gifts come from the Father, but of His own will He brought us forth by the Word of truth (James 1:17–18).
- The Holy Spirit distributes His gifts to whomever He will (1 Cor. 12:1–11).
- God allowed the Israelites to have Saul as a king; God disposed of Saul and replaced him with David. When David had served the purposes of God, he died (Acts 13:21–22, 36).

The implications are staggering. According to the Father's purposes, all gifts come from Him, are distributed by the Holy Spirit, and are used until we complete God's purposes. We are looking straight into the face of a Sovereign God who exercises sovereignty sovereignly! Is there any aspect of our existence over which His purposes have no control?

The mentor is dedicated to assisting the mentoree in finding his or her place in God's economy. We turn now to how we can learn of bestowed value in the mentoree's life.

LEARNING OF BESTOWED VALUE

The mentor assigns nine tasks to discover what has transpired over the years in the mentoree's life. These paint a collage indicating the Father's design and earlier shaping of the mentoree.

Prayer and Fasting

Prayer and fasting heighten sensitivity to God's will, whether through the written Word or the witness of the Spirit. Fasting is the biblical means to humble oneself, and God gives grace to the humble (James 4:6). Through the ages, Christians have sought God's will in private retreat where they fasted for brief to prolonged periods. We often counsel mentorees on the nature of the fast and recommend they seek insight by praying and fasting themselves.

Placement in the Body of Christ

God desires His flock to be fitted with each other and experience the body life of the church. We are in relationship to edify others who benefit from our gifts, inclinations, bents, and talents. As others come to know what our gifts and talents are, the gifts in turn give us an identity familiar to others (Ps. 107:41; Eph. 4:16; 1 Cor. 12). Early in our work with a new mentoree we ask: "When you walk into the room, what is it that people expect from you based on your gifts? What are you known for?"

Personal Prophecy

Personal prophecy can reveal a person's gifts and the manner of their use (1 Tim. 1:18; 4:14). We inquire whether leaders with the gift of prophecy have ministered to the mentoree, and, if so, was there a recording and later a transcription from the recording that was made part of the mentoree's personal journal.

The Church's Leaders

The pastors, elders, and other leaders of the church are likely to have observed the contributions a member of the church has made. We want to know whether these acts of service have some kind of pattern. Was the mentoree encouraged in these contributions, and did older members skilled in the same areas apprentice the mentoree to improve his or her skills? (Eph. 4:11–16; 1 Tim. 5:17; Titus 1:5–9; 1 Pet. 5:1–2, 5).

Godly Family Members

An aunt, uncle, parent, or grandparent may have observed and commented on a young person's particular leanings, not out of the older person's personal aspirations for the child but because he or she had a glimpse of some budding talent or gift. They sensed God working at an early age (Prov. 22:6). We place no age limit on when mentorees may have heard these words of encouragement. Mentorees aged seventy and above have recalled a saintly grandmother commenting on a promising future.

Life's Circumstances

The events of one's life may have been inconsequential or catastrophic, but in God's hands, they are like road signs guiding along some path. They may be crucibles to test a person, or they may be pathways leading to meaningful contributions in behalf of the kingdom. We sometimes assign a well-known biography or autobiography to help stir the imagination of the mentoree regarding his or her own past (Gen. 45:3–9).

The *Rhema* Word

This moment of insight can come during times of meditation. Or it may come merely driving down the road, reading a passage from the Bible, or hearing a single comment from a sermon, book, movie, or song. It produces the proverbial "a-ha." Further counsel may be required, but the *rhema* word may be the start of the journey toward realizing purpose (Rom. 10:17).

Sovereign Epochs

Ancient biblical accounts of difficulties–the flood, the plagues on Egypt, the crossing of the Red Sea, the famine in Egypt, the enslavement in a heathen land, the wanton execution and diasporas of the first-century church—all include men and women who responded with the purposes of God in hand. Today, automobile or aircraft accidents, floods, economic depressions, terrorist devastation, earthquakes, tornadoes, avalanches and mud slides, wars and pogroms, gulags, and concentration camps all produce people notable for spontaneous and remarkable responses in the name of the Lord. God creates the conditions; man arises to the occasion. A veritable goldmine of insight on a person's purpose arises out of the ash heaps of life.

The Autobiography

The Renaissance gave birth to the autobiography as an art form and a revelation of the events and journeys of thousands of people. King David likely was the greatest autobiographer of all time, and the Psalms are adequate testimony to this. In the autobiography, a mentoree searching for calling and purpose can rely on God to provide recall as the autobiography takes shape. We discover God, and ourselves, in the act of writing. We require all mentors to write an autobiography, to provide a chronological picture of where they have been and what they have done. We also require all mentorees to complete their writing with two to three needs they want addressed or goals they want to achieve in the mentoring relationship. An added utility of the autobiographies is that we use them to match mentor with mentoree.

We ask all new mentorees to complete a questionnaire that addresses all nine of these "memory shakers." They have produced results for people of all ages and from all walks of life.

It is a thrill to administer the questionnaire to an older person. Years ago they had a dream, a "burn," or that proverbial urge, but it was submerged into forgetfulness because of the usual events of life, starting a family or career, buying and paying for a home, putting the kids through college, or caring for an ill parent. Purpose had been lost, or so the older adult thought. And then we come along, always assigning an older mentor to those of similar age, and we saw a thrilling event—first the blade, then the sprout, the young sapling, and a rediscovered purpose rising to its own place in the kingdom. Purpose never dies. Life's vicissitudes may have covered it, but by His grace, our Father resurrects and reestablishes it.

CHAPTER FIVE

Transitions in Mentoree Growth 1: Personal and Interpersonal Changes

I WORK IN WOODS, NOT AS A MASTER CRAFTSMAN BUT AS A HOBBYIST WHO OVER THE YEARS HAS ACQUIRED A DEEP AFFECTION FOR WOOD— ROSEWOOD, REDWOOD, OLIVE ASH BURL, BIRD'S EYE MAPLE, OAK, walnut, Carpathian elm, and more. Once I commit myself to a particular plank, block, or veneer of wood, I accept its history. The craftsman envisions the unfolding unique beauty of the finished product by accepting the wood's personal history. Mentoring, like working wood, is a process of discovery. The craftsman is a collaborator, taking hidden beauty and often scars and exposing them, knowing there is a difference between "perfection" and "beauty." The craftsman, as artist, seeks beauty without sacrificing structural integrity, but perfection is an illusion. Mentoring is all of these and more.

PERSONAL HISTORY AS FOUNDATION FOR GROWTH

Mentorees, like trees, have a history that mentors cannot deny, avoid, or reject. The history contains lean as well as fat years, joyful and sad times, scars, and a unique genetic structure. In all of us, personal history is likened to geologic layers, formed of some distant and sometimes cataclysmic past. These "layers," then, are never known for what they are until they slip unexpectedly into one's conversation as a stutter, nervous twitch, or emotional outburst. These events of the past are like built-in video tapes that remain sometimes for many years. The mentoree does not forget them, and because of them, the mentor eventually discovers more of whom he or she is working with. The task of the mentor is to assist in turning history into beauty. The Cross's message is one of restoration, and mentor is the human manager of that process.

Mentors, like Carl Jung when he replied to his student, are less likely to be disappointed with those they mentor when they too have learned their lessons and do not become disillusioned. Such mentors are also more accepting of them as individuals even though they may not approve of all their past or present behavior. There is, moreover, no perfect mentor any more than there are perfect mentorees. God achieves His purposes by bringing imperfection together with imperfection.

The biblical record serves us well in describing what God's people were before they came to Christ. They too had flotsam of the past as they entered the new life in Christ.

Did the apostle Paul ever recover from the "body of this death" with which he struggled? (Rom. 7:24). Did he shake from his memory his part in Stephen's (Acts 8:1–2) murder and thereafter his rejection of John Mark? (Acts 15:36–39). Why do various writers refer to Peter as the apostle who limped? Did he recover from the embarrassment and guilt connected with his denials? (Matt. 26:69–75). Consider Moses: Was there a subconscious connection between his impatient smashing of the rock a second time and his impetuous murdering of the Egyptian guard (Exod. 2:11–12)?

The new birth transfers us from our past into Christ. In Christ, we become righteous. In Christ, we are free of condemnation. In Christ, we pass from death to life. In Christ, we are separate from sin. In Christ and by His work on the Cross, we are adopted into the family of God, we are justified, and all things are made right. In Christ, we are a new creation; all things become new. In Christ, we have an inheritance among the saints. In Christ, we sit with Him in the heavens. In Christ, we look forward to a place prepared for us in His Father's house with its many mansions.

All of these mark transitions from past to present, and they promise further transitions as the gospel carves out its history in our lives. Daily, the old passes away, and daily, everything becomes new. The mentoree comes to the mentor with a history that continues to unfold.

DISCIPLES: THE RAW MATERIAL OF MENTORING

Shortly after becoming Christians, new believers begin the journey in Christ and are introduced to the process of discipleship, which, as I have already stated, usually includes basic doctrine, learning new behavior, and character development. I have chosen this trilogy because this is what I believe characterizes the majority of church-based discipling programs.

Doctrine

Six elementary doctrinal issues are identified in Hebrews 6:1–2, and in the early church these were pivotal: repentance from dead works, faith toward God, instructions about washings, laying on of hands, resurrection of the dead, and eternal judgment. These have expanded, as church history shows, and vary in terms of denominational preferences. Before the 1960s, discipling included the essential doctrines taught by the evangelical streams of the church. Lutherans got a good dose of "grace"; Presbyterians learned of "predestination"; and Baptist converts had drummed into them the finer points of being "born again" and of "personal salvation."

Character and obedience, however, are not mastered through didactic exercises.

Additional doctrines appeared during the Charismatic Renewal of the 1960s. These included baptism in the Holy Spirit, gifts of the Spirit, worship, healing, and spiritual warfare.

Obedience and Character Development

Starting with the fourth chapter of Ephesians and for the remainder of his letter, Paul provides numerous prescriptions for obedient behavior (Eph. 4:1, 17; 5:8, 10, 17, 19, 20, 22; 6:1, 4, 8, 10). The fruit of the Holy Spirit cited in Galatians 5:22–23 are frequently referred to as the essentials of Christian character— love, joy, peace, gentleness, goodness, longsuffering, meekness, and others.

Obedience and character development are reciprocal events, and it would be helpful if young disciples learned about them in this way. Character emerges out of repeated acts of obedience;

developed character, in turn, becomes the driving force for continuing obedience. Character and obedience, however, are not mastered through didactic exercises. The critical remarks of Gordon MacDonald apply here:

> What passes for people development [inappropriately] happens in a classroom, and the certification of a person is by diploma from an institution rather than the stamp of approval from an overseer. . . . The criteria for judgment of people usually [and wrongly] rests upon knowledge rather than wisdom, achievement rather than character, profit rather than creativity.[1]

One does not become a disciple by graduating with straight A's from a seminar whose subject matter is Christian doctrine, character, and behavior. Consider again Robert Coleman's observations that only personal attention, much as a father gives his children, build men and women. This is not a matter of proxy by some organization or class. Coleman does not use the term *mentor*, but the implication is clear; only people who lead can prepare others for service. Short of this, "it is no wonder about half of those who make professions and join the church eventually fall away or lose the glow of Christian experience, and fewer still grow in sufficient knowledge and grace to be of any real service to the Kingdom."[2]

GRADUATION FROM DISCIPLING

The first half of Jesus' ministry addressed doctrine (the kingdom of God), obedience to His words (". . . he who has my commandments and keeps them"), and character development (the Sermon on the Mount). Jesus expanded the conditions for following Him during the second half of His ministry and taught His disciples how to carry out ministry. These included meeting human and personal needs—feeding the hungry, healing the sick, driving out demons—and understanding the circumstances in which prayer and fasting were necessary to accomplish their goals. He placed limitations on whom they were to speak to and how much to say. He made them accountable, requiring reports on each missionary journey. The shift to spending more time with the disciples was a sign He was preparing them for a higher order of service. The apostle John's model of maturity illustrated the kind of transition implicit in Jesus' training.

John's Model of Increasing Maturity

The apostle was about one hundred years old when he wrote his first letter. By this time, he had walked in the steps of the Master for about seventy years. His readers would take his words seriously. He addresses all believers as children (of God) in their generic sense (1 John 2:1, 12, 28; 3:7, 18; 4:4; 5:21), as he does in John 13:33 and as does Paul (Gal. 4:19). However, John addresses the youngest members in the family of God metaphorically as children who are deficient in spiritual understanding (1 John 2:13, 18; 1 Cor. 14:20). He addresses the young men in 1 John 2:13–14, whom Vine refers to as the "second branch of the spiritual family."[3] Fathers, on the other hand, are those who have advanced knowledge of Christ (1 John 2:13–14).[4]

John admits of the spiritually immature children their knowledge of the Father and warns of antichrists. To the young men, he commends their strength in having fought with and overcome the evil one. To the fathers, he acknowledges their having known the Father from the beginning. Spiritual maturity is graded, so that even the youngest of disciples (children who know some doctrine about the evil one) are separated from those prepared for more difficult mentoring, who, we infer, are the young men who have faced threats and temptations and won. They too, when they were immature, knew about the antichrists, but they took their lessons seriously, and when confronted with a fight, they had come home victorious. From John, we learn an important principle about readiness. Acorns, referenced earlier as undeveloped believers, are the same as John's immature children. They would not be eligible for the mentoring program.

Failing in Spiritual Growth

The writer of Hebrews indicts immature Christians who have failed to learn and follow doctrine and thereby need further instruction in elementary principles, saying that without having practiced doctrine, their senses are not trained to discern good and evil (Heb. 5:12–13). Paul echoes this in his reference to believers tossed about by every wind of doctrine, who are easily deceived (1 Cor. 14:20; Eph. 4:14–15).

Failing in Character Development

R. C. Sproul writes that holiness derives from the development of character—the fruit of the Spirit identified in Galatians 5:22–23.[5] Paul's discussion of character in 1 Corinthians 13 concludes with a comment on his own development—that as a child he exhibited behavior that is best described by *eros*. (Paul's correction of the church members in Corinth focused on *eros*, which was an apt description of their religious behavior.) When he became an adult, in contrast, he put on *agape*. Paul also wrote in Galatians 5:19–21 that those engaged in fleshly behavior would not inherit the kingdom of God, which (in my thesis) prevented them from pursuing calling and purpose in a mentoring relationship.

Failing in Obedience

Disciples must learn to live under the authority of those who disciple them before they can be responsible for the more advanced requirements of mentoring. Jesus said there might be those who do all kinds of spiritual works and still fail to live under the Father's authority, and this disqualifies them from the kingdom (Matt. 7:21–23).

TRANSITIONS DURING MENTORING

Change seldom occurs in a bubble free of social, psychological, behavioral, and spiritual challenges. Natural and spiritual changes are intertwined so that both the sacred and the profane can glorify God. I do not believe spiritual growth is possible without corresponding behavioral change. I do not believe behavioral change long endures without the heart of man also changing. The Bible is clear that man is a complex composite— a "wholistic" creature—and mind, soul, and spirit work in tandem. Modern science and the "naturalistic method" may have compartmentalized humans into parts, but God listens to the words coming out of a person's mouth and follows them back to their source—the heart.

Growth Is a Process of Becoming

The telescope's optics reach out and grab the image of some distant object and bring it to where the observer stands. The telescope transcends the time required to travel to the observed object, and it transcends the space between the object and its image. The telescope enables us to see space and time in a different dimension. Our journey in Christ is teleological, and Paul (using the original Greek words from which we get the word telescope) describes this in Philippians 3:12, 15.

> Not that I have already obtained it, or have already *become perfect*, but I press on in order that I may lay hold of that for which also I was laid hold of by Christ Jesus . . . Brethren, I do not regard myself as having laid hold of it yet; but one thing I do: forgetting what lies behind and reaching forward to what lies ahead, I press on toward the goal for the prize of the upward call of God in Christ Jesus. Let us therefore, as many as *are perfect*, have this attitude. (Emphases added)

Paul uses two forms of the word *perfect*. A paraphrase of verse 12 goes this way: "I am in the process of perfecting what Christ laid hold of me to do." A paraphrase of verse 15 would read: "Those of us who already are perfect in God's sight press on toward our goals." Paul looks through the telescope into the future and sees his goal—the completed perfected work of which he is a part. To God, he is already perfect. Paul, nevertheless, is a realist. He turns from the telescope to the mirror (you will recall—the one that was darkened and obscured a clear image) and looks at himself struggling daily. He sees himself in the step-by-step process of perfecting that which, in God's sight, time, and space, is already a perfected and accomplished fact. The teleological model is at the heart of the transitions that mentors observe to measure the growth of mentorees. The mentor looks at the mentoree and sees him or her in the here and now, but he or she has been given a glimpse by the Father of what the mentoree is to become when living out his or her divine purpose. Nevertheless, there is a journey from the *being perfected* to the *perfect*. Three personal and interpersonal processes are associated with the transitions, and they help in our understanding of it. These pertain to the way transition affects how the mentoree responds to friends and family, to the dynamic relation of hope, faith, and love as presented by Paul in 1 Corinthians 13, and to the challenges of jealousy and envy.

Transition, Predictability, and Challenges

Behavioral scientists speak of *desocialization*. This involves setting aside, departing from, removing, disengaging, or unlearning ways of the past. Personal growth involves many instances of desocialization. The young child puts aside (often with considerable help from his or her parents) childish ways as he or she approaches and enters adolescence. Newly married grooms hopefully will be desocialized from "bachelor ways" when assuming the responsibilities of husband and provider. The religious convert learns that in Christ, "old things are passed away," and the time has come to quit running with the old gang and to rid oneself of certain habits and thought patterns. Desocialization, while common among religious converts, equally applies to those who have experienced political and psychotherapeutic conversions, as well as other major changes during the course of a lifetime.

The movement toward new ways of acting and thinking is *resocialization*, or relearning. While desocialization signifies that "old things pass away," resocialization signifies that "all things are becoming new" (1 Cor. 5:17). When Paul tells his readers to "put on Christ," he is talking about resocialization.

Two aspects of major life changes are important to mentoring programs. The first is that desocialization and resocialization usually occur at the same time. The second is that people undergoing change become unpredictable to those closest to them.

Concurrent desocialization and resocialization
Concurrent desocialization and resocialization creates problems. Consider Paul's instructions to the thief to cease stealing,

get a job, and earn a surplus, so that he can give to others who have a need (Eph. 4:28). He agrees to stop stealing and is given a job, but all the while he thinks of his thrill-filled days as a thief. New behavior and old thoughts are where resocialization and desocialization overlap. Consider the alcoholic who Paul tells to stop drinking and be filled instead with the Spirit. He agrees, but during times of prayer and praise, the desire for the next drink remains (Eph. 4:18). Sobriety and the urge to binge coexist.

Both the thief and the drinker want to change; they become disciples. However, desocialization and resocialization occur simultaneously, and to the person who experiences them, they are opposing forces. The concurrent laying-off and putting-on is emotionally disturbing. Emotional conflict is not the sign of a moral failing. It is a natural consequence of change! These people are neither fish nor foul. They live in a social psychological limbo, neither here nor there. While identity, at this point, may be problematic, there is little question that personal crisis is not. This happens in mentoring relationships, and mentors are required to be sensitive to the dynamics.

Take the example of Rob. He was highly recommended by the pastor of his church to enter the mentoring program. He had been in a junior ministry position, and the church's leaders anticipated a great future for him. Rob had a responsible job as a computer system integrator for a large local corporation. The mentor assigned tasks that would move Rob toward more effective ministry, but as they got more acquainted, the mentor discovered Rob had a problem with pornography. Each day after lunch, he visited the porn web sites. The wise mentor then asked Rob about his wife's anxiety and depression, neither of which Rob had mentioned, but which are common among wives whose husbands are porn addicts. Surprised that the mentor had this kind of insight, Rob was disarmed but receptive to counsel. He and the mentor agreed he could remain in the mentoring program only if he accepted an assignment of desocialization from inappropriate behavior and concurrent resocialization as a husband and future participant in ministry. Rob wanted ministry, but it would be his only if he were willing to grab hold of and choke the sin. Resocialization was contingent on desocialization, and Rob was "caught" in the crossfire wondering if he could hang on long enough to finish the course.

Rob was fortunate to have a mentor team standing alongside him. The younger member of the team, Dan, was Rob's age. He also was a computer specialist. Dan asked Rob when he usually visited the porn sites, and when told it was after lunch each day, Dan had a ready prescription for change. Rob was to call his wife immediately after lunch each day and tell her he loved her (reso-cialization). Then, he was to call Dan and assure him he had remained clean for that day (desocialization). In three weeks, pornography disappeared, and purpose-oriented mentoring began.

Change and loss of predictability

The second inconvenience connected with change is that the mentoree becomes unpredictable. He is a new person. His wife, parents, and the guys at the office or in the morning fellowship do not know how to interact with him anymore. To be unpre-dictable causes anxiety and sometimes fear in others and threatens them. For, after all, the mentoree experiencing change is a different kind of person. The closer others are to the person who changes, the more the change affects them. My perception of you and my association with you have enjoyed a consistency up until the present time. If you change however, you force a change in how I see and respond to you. Mentorees, by definition, are in a growth period. Growth is change. The mentoree is pursuing new goals, solving problems, meeting needs, achieving his or her purposes in God, and the fire in his or her eyes does not easily adapt to the old light and shadows. One of the most familiar examples of this is the person who first becomes a Christian and changes his or her lifestyle (1 Pet. 2:11–12; 3:14; 4:3–4).

Unpredictability is a staple in the life of one experiencing change, and the mentor needs to know how to handle it.

Acquaintances, friends, and family of the mentoree may feel neglected or rejected. The mentoree has God's calling on his or her life. Skills and talents are coming together. The mentoree focuses more on God's calling and takes less time with activities that earlier preoccupied him or her. Distaff readers will remember when they attended an inspiring Christian Business Women's Club or Aglow conference and came home with new vision. Down from the mountain they came, singing and praising God, and husbands wondered what happened to wives they no longer recognized. Or, consider the men. They return home from a Promise Keepers rally committed to loving wife and children, serving pastor and church, and dedicated to community and improved race relations. They have jumped three levels in devotion to God and country. Wives have not seen such change before. Unpredictability is a staple in the life of one experiencing change, and the mentor needs to know how to handle it, reassuring the mentoree that change and unpredictability are not moral failings.

Transition, Faith, Hope, and Love

First Corinthians 13 concludes with the familiar "But now abide faith, hope, love, these three, but the greatest of these is love" (v. 13). What a treasure chest of insight this is for the mentor and the mentoree!

Love is the *agape* of earlier discussions. *Agape* bestows value. The content of value is the calling and purposes of God in our lives. Unfortunate is the person who begins a journey independent of a purpose based on conferred value. A life of frustration results under these circumstances, and God is not constrained to give grace to accomplish purposes other than His own. Paul admonishes Timothy to remain fixed on God's purposes for his life (2 Tim. 1:6, 9).

Faith and hope each lie on either side of love. On the right is the object of faith or the perfected dimension of the journey (Phil. 3:15); on the left is hope or the perfecting dimension (Phil. 3:12).

Christians have faith in the finality of God's provision and promises, including His purposes for them. Road maps give assurance (before the fact) that we will arrive at our destination, which is the object of faith. Within the mentoring enterprise, this object is purpose bestowed on us through *agape*.

Hope, on the other hand, is in close association with the challenges to and the energy for completing the journey. Hope does not exist apart from at least the prospects of a challenged journey. Few of us have set out on a journey where unforeseen events have not taken place. The car breaks down; we wander off course; we inadvertently detour onto an isolated road that leads to nowhere; a child begins to run a fever; or the kids run out of M&Ms and have a sugar fit. All the time we are heading toward our destination. We laugh. However, the threats can be more dramatic. We lose our job; the marketplace in which we have been selling our products dries up; or an employee sues the company and causes a lengthy lawsuit. In our churches, the worship leader runs off with the pianist just before the start of a major conference. The senior elder or deacon starts an insurrection threatening a church split right at the time a major fund-raising campaign is to begin. Anything can occur and obstruct as we journey toward some specific God-given goal in which we have great faith. Faith has not disappeared, but it is now less certain.

Hope enters at the point of a threat. It is the attitude that pushes the sojourner on in the face of trouble, all the time continuing in awareness and assurance of the goal in which there is faith. The threat, challenge, or digression hides the final destination from view. For forty years, Moses had hope he was to lead the Israelites out of Egypt, and for another forty years he crisscrossed the desert still visualizing with the eye of faith the Promised Land. Faith saw Israel's inheritance; hope drove Moses and the Israelites toward it.

Hope increases each time there is a victory, in the same way successively heavier weights build the power lifter's muscle. Some writers have described *habit strength* as a quality of hope. Hope increased by overcoming challenges possesses habit strength. Mentoree's confidence increases as habit strength increases. For all the reasons others may give for the purposes of suffering and disappointment, the behavioral scientist sees these as opportunities to increase hope and to optimize one's habit strength (Rom. 5:5; 12:12; 1 Cor. 9:10).

If there is no suffering, there is no habit strength. No threats along the journey and no challenges lend no occasion to build strength to complete the course. Faith and hope are teleological relatives. Hope is the perfecting dimension of the journey. Faith is the perfected dimension. Hope and faith, however, have absolutely no reason to exist short of conferred calling and purpose.

Why among the three, then, is *agape* the greatest? Because *agape* is the reason for the journey. *Agape* is the source of the mentoree's calling and purpose and therefore the condition in which hope and faith operate spiritually and behaviorally in the life of the mentoree. This insight is one of the most significant tools the mentor has, and I have found it to have transforming value for most of the mentors I have trained as well.

Transition, Success, and Envy's Threat

Mentorees who accept the challenge and chase the high calling of God are likely to experience the envy of others, particularly as they get closer to their goal. Successful Christians are disconcerting to their peers who are not making the grade or have yet to start the journey! Enter envy.

Envy is the "displeasure produced by witnessing or hearing of the advantage or prosperity of others; [an] evil sense always attaches to this word . . . [Envy] desires to deprive another of what he has."[6] It differs from jealousy, which, at a lower level of intensity, desires to have the same sort of thing for itself that another has (see, as examples, Matt. 27:18; Mark 15:10; Rom. 1:29; Gal. 5:21; Phil. 1:15; 1 Tim. 6:4; Titus 3:3; 1 Pet. 2:1).

Envy begins by making a comparison. It not only wants to be a mentoree; it seeks to be the mentoree in the place of the one who already is. Envy lets it be known, directly or indirectly, to the envied mentoree: he or she "now is too good to associate with the rest of us"; he or she "doesn't deserve the attention of a mentor"; he or she "was unfairly chosen by the mentor rather than I"; or he or she "is getting too spiritual."[7]

The strategies mentorees use to avert envy are called "envy avoidance." Envy avoidance is the envied person's effort to divert envy that seeks to control. The envied mentoree may say, "It was nothing; I was just lucky," or "I'm really not that good; they had an extra opening, and I happened to be there at just the right time." In more severe cases of envy avoidance, the mentoree may purposefully fail the course or quit and become "one of the guys" again.

Envy's danger for the church is that those who are succeeding may acquiesce and cease the journey, and they too would lose their place in the kingdom to the extent they forsook their calling and purposes in God.

CHAPTER SIX

Transitions in Mentoree Growth 2:
The Emotions of Change

THE PRESENT ERA OF POSTMODERNISM HAS ALERTED US TO INCREASED GNOSTICISM (THE ASSERTED POSSESSION OF SUPERIOR KNOWLEDGE), MYSTICISM, SPIRITUALISM, AND FEELINGS AS EXPLANATIONS OF humankind's behavior and search for God. Using the tripartite model of how we fellowship with God in chapter 1, *eros* best describes these inclinations. The emphasis on emotions and related behavior by postmodernists is not the reason I have included this section as an additional study of the transitions in a mentoree's life. I am not a postmodernist. My rationale is simply that a casual glance through a Bible concordance quickly reveals that emotions and sentiments are common in the Scriptures. Included emotions are fear, horror, dread, anxiety, terror, despair, relief, hope, panic, anger, doubt, depression, and others.

THE EMOTIONS

The interest shown in the role of emotions in behavior has exploded in recent years. Philosopher Aaron Ben-Ze'ev of the University of Haifa, Israel, recognizes the controversial role of emotions in the moral domain.[1] My discussion throughout this book has been a moral discussion: Does the Christian pursue God's purposes for his or her life or not? "Two central features of emotions," writes Ben Ze'-ev, "are particularly problematic for the integration of emotions into the moral domain . . ." The first of these is that emotions are not deliberate; they cannot be predicted. Yet we suddenly recognize them after the fact and then make an effort to tie preceding events to the emotions we experience. The second feature is the partial nature of emotions; they never perfectly represent the impartial nature of morality. We admit to the limited utility of emotions. Nevertheless, we find them helpful in guiding and counseling our mentorees. Therefore, we put forth five guiding premises based on the Bible's references to them:

- Emotions are meaningful in Scripture only when studied in the context in which they occur, and they are subject to the standard rules of biblical interpretation.
- Emotions are an intentional part of God's design for man.
- Emotions are an occurrence of everyday life. They are not contrary to the faith life. In themselves, they do not indicate a moral failing when they are negative, and they are not indicative of "spiritual success" when they provide pleasure.
- Emotions can be negative, positive, accurate, or deceptive, and in their varied expressions are useful as signals of where mentorees are in their goal-seeking behavior.
- Emotions appear in predictable sequences and have value in describing and explaining goal-oriented behavior.

A good friend whom I had known for many years called from his home in another state. He was a committed Christian, fairly well acquainted with Scripture, and his wife was a well-known prayer warrior whose counsel was frequently sought by younger women. The couple had their act together. I had mentored him on occasions, and I had a good understanding of the course his life had taken. The desperation in his voice when he first called concerned me, so I skipped the usual niceties and gave him a wide berth to share why he had called. At the time, I was writing the first edition of this book and had just completed this chapter. (I have to make clear, however, that the materials for this section have been in development and undergone testing for at least thirty years.) Here is what he said: "I don't know what's happening. Ballistic is the best word to describe what is going on. It's as if I am experiencing anxiety, anger, depression, and fear all at the same time and then bouncing back and forth, first one, and then the other. This is weird. Can you help?"

I asked how his management consulting business was doing, to which he replied that it was progressing but nothing to warrant bragging. I then told him I was going to ask him one question, and that he was to call me back as soon as he had the answer. Twenty-four hours later, he called back, said he had the answer, and that as soon as he had the answer every emotion he had been experiencing was gone. Later in this chapter, I will tell what the question was and what his answer was.

The mentor needs to know something about transitions in mentoree growth, and he or she benefits from knowing the role emotions play in that growth. This certainly is true when the definitions of the emotions relate to the circumstances in which the mentorees find themselves. The Bible has much to say about this.

In this discussion of emotions, my concern is only with how they relate to goal-seeking behavior. I am not concerned with their relation to metabolic disturbances or endocrine imbalances; with malaise associated with illness, pain, or disability; with toxic or neurological pathology; or with the side effects of medications or other mood-altering substances such as caffeine, sugar, nicotine, alcohol, or illicit drugs.

Emotions are internal road signs marking an additional level of response to whatever we are thinking or doing outwardly. As road signs, they are an additional piece of evidence of how the mentoree is proceeding on his or her pilgrim's journey.

Figure 1 on the following page assists in understanding how changing circumstances give rise to one emotion or another. The built-in assumption to this model is that there is a predictable sequence for the appearance of emotions.

Each of the first four emotions in the flowchart has three possibilities, indicating its presence, absence, or removal. The failure to remove the circumstances leading to an emotion results in the next emotion in the diagram. Hence, failure to remove a distraction leads to anxiety, anxiety leads to fear, and fear to anger. Once the circumstances giving rise to an emotion disappear, there is relief.

Doubt

Doubt is not a weakness of faith but rather the absence of faith. He who doubts is not yet ready to begin the journey. Some

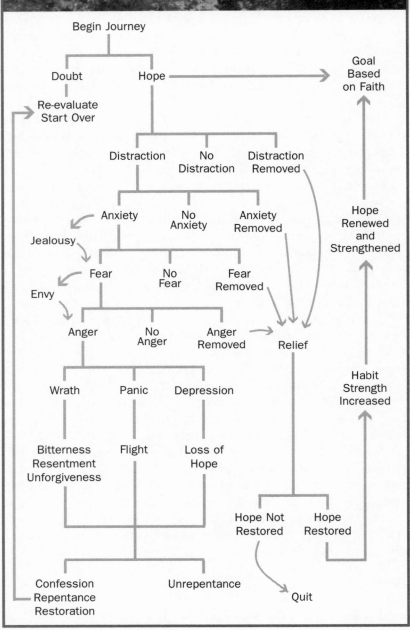

Figure 1

people have a difficult time making a decision; others weigh an option and then draw back. Whatever the reasons, it is clear the mentoree is ill-prepared to proceed. The mentor merely encourages the mentoree to refocus and establish certainty of purpose. To doubt, James says, is to waver (1:6). It also means to "stand in two ways" (Matt. 13:31), or to be uncertain as to direction (Matt. 28:17). The mentoree would benefit from either personal counseling or repeating the beginning discipling course.

Hope

I introduced hope in chapter 5. I discuss it below in order to compare it with relief. Hope is the emotion or sentiment with which we begin the journey. It is the physical, mental, or emotional reserve pushing us forward, in pursuit of our purposes. Hope is what "happens" when someone compliments or encourages us. It happens when we step on the scales, see that we weigh ten pounds less, and know we can run the race just a bit faster or reach aerobic capacity on the treadmill.

Persistent and heightened hope "theoretically," as we show in figure 1, takes mentorees directly to the goal in which they have faith. Most of us do not have this privilege because, as the Bible makes clear, suffering and challenges work to our greater advantage.

Distraction

Distraction is not an emotion. It is the physical or mental digression away from the object of our faith. If doubt is to "stand in two ways," then digression is to take a path other than the right one. Ten of the spies sent to reconnoiter the Promised Land saw the milk, honey, luscious clusters of grapes, waving heads of grain, rolling pastures, and sparkling streams everywhere. God had prepared a good place for Israel. Nevertheless, they took their eyes off the prize. Once the giants distracted them, the spies made note of their stature, their armament, the ferocity of their countenance, and the manner in which they marched without breaking rank. The ten became experts on giants, no longer focusing their attention on God's provision. They were distracted.

Mentors know distractions for mentorees come in many forms: preoccupation with health, appearance, or financial resources, the envy of others, or scheduling difficulties. We live in a society that endlessly competes for every person's attention and loyalty. The marketplace performs its first duty through distraction. Hundreds of competitors, secular and religious alike, stand at our doors knocking and saying, "Come with us." We do not need money to be attractive to those who vie for our loyalty; the volunteering of discretionary time is sufficient. Volunteerism is a money-equivalent; the more volunteers enrolled, the less the depletion of bank reserves.

Of my friend, the management consultant referred to above, I asked the question: "When did you first become distracted from your principle goal?" His answer, twenty-four hours later, was: "It's spooky. I was distracted just before all those crazy emotions began to pour over me."

Anxiety

While distraction takes the primary attention off the prize, the prize nevertheless remains present in some degree in the mind of the mentoree. How much in the mentoree's mind? Just enough to threaten loss of the prize, and this is the emotion of anxiety.

Anxiety is the emotion of perceived potential loss. The mentor seeks the reason for anxiety and finds it in distraction. He or she acts to remove the distraction, exposing it for what it is and the effect it has had on the mentoree.

Anxiety is the early stage of fear. Figure 1 illustrates how unrelieved anxiety becomes fear. In Matthew 6, Jesus encourages His disciples six times not to be anxious. Here is the Lord of creation, and He had a name for how His disciples were acting. He did not give them a lecture on "anxiety is sin" or "you of little faith."

Consider the circumstances. He recruits twelve commoners and tells them they will be part of a new government: The kingdom is within you; the kingdom has come; seek first the kingdom. Perhaps He shared this news while they were standing in view of the courtyard of the Roman garrison. He had said they would have clothes, food, and shelter. They were to focus on the kingdom, and here they were standing at the door of the garrison. In one corner of the courtyard was a pile of rusty nails—the kind used for crucifixions. Perhaps the day before they passed other would-be insurrectionists, now impaled on Roman crosses. The sight, groans, and stench of bodies rotting in the Mediterranean sun were still fresh in their minds. In the center of the courtyard was a whipping post on which hung the whip, each strand containing sharp stones and nails capable of tearing hunks of flesh from the victim's back. Jesus invites them to follow Him. The Twelve had reason to be anxious. Standing between them and the kingdom of God was the Roman garrison and a vigilant government that acted quickly to quell any group hinting at insurrection. Many roaming messiahs had promised, tried, and failed. They too ended up on the roadside crosses.

This was quite a distraction, indeed, and with each assessment of it, the anxiety mounted. There was the potential loss of a heavenly kingdom that they did not yet understand, and the greater potential loss of their lives. Following Jesus' intensive training, assignments, miracles, doctrine, and resurrection, it still took Pentecost to make them bold enough to proclaim the new government in public.

Paul twice had to do damage control in reminding Timothy not to waver, lose faith, or neglect his purpose in life (1 Tim. 4:14; 2 Tim. 1:6–14). Paul reminded his beloved Philippians: "Be anxious for nothing, but in everything by prayer and supplication with thanksgiving let your requests be known to God. And the peace of God which surpasses all comprehension, shall guard your hearts and minds [read: reduce your anxiety] in Christ Jesus" (Phil. 4:6–7). Paul's prescription was that they concentrate on whatever is true, honorable, right, pure, lovely, and of good repute. Minds dwelling on these things would experience the God of Peace. It is a passage filled with rich meaning.

One's thoughts are more likely to influence the behavior directly following those thoughts. Athletes control anxiety by visualization. Visualization blocks out distractions that give rise to anxiety. Mentors who have not lost sight of the mentoree's purposes in God draw four anxiety-reducing principles from Philippians 4:6–9.

- Prayer and supplication. Confess the distraction and ask for forgiveness that it took your eye off the preferred prize. Recommit to your purposes in God. Prayer brings the mentoree into the presence of the Father; supplication is the posture of humility before Him. God gives grace to the humble, meaning that He supernaturally provides the will and power to recommit and perform what is necessary.
- Thankfulness. Be thankful to the Father. Develop a written list of all you are thankful for and verbally recite these day

after day. Autobiographical thankfulness recaptures that part of the past that brings the mentoree back to the present and reaffirms his or her journey.

- Petition. Ask God for renewed vision of what He has given you. Ask for new illumination from the Scriptures so you can be obedient to them. A petition made in behalf of God's calling and purposes for the mentoree is obviously within His will, hence, we know He hears and answers (1 John 5:14–15).
- Thought life. Mentally embrace and dwell on all that is honorable, right, pure, lovely, and of good repute. The practice of this prevents further distractions and therefore alleviates anxiety.

These practices first produce relief and then return us to renewed hope. The habit strength of hope has increased by virtue of the fact that the mentoree has acquired a new set of skills for responding to future instances of anxiety.

Relief is not the only place anxiety may reach. On the left side of Figure 1, I have included an alternate path—jealousy. Jesus left little doubt the disciples would have clothing, food, and shelter, but veiled His assurances in metaphors—lilies of the field, birds feeding on grain, and foxes with their holes—that may have eluded them. For a fleeting moment, the disciples thought of their compatriots continuing in their income-generating pursuits, wondering why they had all the good things in life while the disciples had no promise of the same. Comparison led to jealousy. Unabated, jealousy increases the chance that fear will follow anxiety. This was not the only time Jesus put choices before them: "The one who puts his hands to the plow cannot look back"; "Count the cost before you decide to follow me"; and "If you are controlled by family, ambition, or material goods, you cannot be my disciples."

The opposite of agape is not hate, as some would suggest. It is fear.

Fear

Fear follows and is an extension of unrelieved anxiety. It is not enough that anxiety immobilizes us; fear focuses on that which causes the anxiety. Anxiety, as the precursor to fear, rises to a higher level of intensity, and many Bible references attest to our susceptibility and inability to control it.

Fear is intimidation by enemies or some object of dread or terror. In Scripture, according to Vine, the word in the original suggests cowardice, timidity, or fearfulness. Our concern is "fear of loss" of a desired goal.

John examines fear and love together. "There is no fear in love; but perfect love casts out fear, because fear involves punishment, and the one who fears is not perfected by love" (1 John 4:19). The mentor spells out for the mentoree the connection between these two.

- Why is there no fear in love? Love is the source of the goal and makes it visible to us as the object of faith. John tells us the two cannot coexist.
- Why does perfect love cast out fear? Perfected *agape* is as God sees it in its completed state. Seeing the goal as an accomplished fact denies the possibility of a fear of loss.
- Why does fear involve punishment? Fear signals loss of God-given value. Fear is deprivation from divine plan and purpose. God creates us for purpose. To take the analogy one step further, hell is separation from the purposes He intended us to have.
- Why is not the one who fears perfected in *agape*? Because fear resulting from distraction turns its back on God's purposes, goes astray, and loses sight of what love produces. The opposite of *agape* is not hate, as some would suggest. It is fear.

Fear can lead to either anger or panic. Anger is proactive and strikes out to destroy whatever it is that causes fear. Panic is not proactive and flees whatever it is that causes the fear.

Even as anxiety can give rise to jealousy, so also fear, rather than resulting in relief, can lead to envy. The jealous mentoree only wants his or her share of the good life—clothes, food, and shelter. He or she did not covet what others owned. Anger is stronger than anxiety and strong enough to produce envy. As the threat of loss increases, envy viciously strikes out in anger and wants to take possession of what others have or, worse, wants to destroy them.

Anger

Anger says: "Fear has awakened me, and it is insufficient for the task at hand. It will not solve the problem." Hence, fear is a

wake-up call, converts to anger, and anger attacks that which
prevents continuation of the journey. Anger strikes out and seeks
to destroy, maim, or remove the obstruction to progress. The
obstruction comes in many forms. It may be a taciturn colleague
refusing to carry his weight on a joint project. An unsympathetic
spouse who still has not "caught the vision." The devil or demons
that continue to badger me and rob me of my inheritance in God.
Certain members of the church who refuse to support a new
construction project or missionary ministry. I may be the
problem: putting forth too little effort or having a wrong focus,
being overweight or failing in strength because I exercise too
little, recognizing character defects, or holding to inaccurate
stereotypes. Anger is aroused, and it strikes out.

Scripture identifies two kinds of anger—inner and outward.
The strongest of all angers is the wrath of man (Eph. 4:31; Col.
3:8; 1 Tim. 2:8; James 1:19–20). Wrath is outward and strikes in
revenge at the cause of anger. It seeks to destroy. Inner anger,
while seething, can rise up quickly but just as quickly subside
(Luke 4:28; Acts 19:28; Rom. 2:8).

The intensity of anger to remove obstructions is proportional
to how intensely we feel about our goals. They are mirror images
of each other. Point to the person who is driven, compulsive,
dogged, and unreserved in pursuing his or her purposes in God,
and that person's anger will match his or her passion for achieving
goals. The greater the vision, the greater the rage over thwarted
vision. Why is this so, and how does it apply to mentorees?

Consider again the thrust of chapter 4 on calling, purpose, and
destiny. What level of intensity must Moses have had when he set
out on the forty-year trip across the desert? In the early Christian
era, few matched Paul's intensity of purpose. Jesus set his face
toward Jerusalem, knowing the requirements of the task before He
eventually ascended Calvary. These men were driven. Blood and
sweat compose the ink in which the history of the church is written.
Many of us have known driven men and women, and we have
witnessed how they flare up when they confront obstructions to
their goals. How much of this is a character defect? Is the failure
of composure a sin? God will judge, but one thing is certain. Every
Christian soul is pregnant with divine DNA, and it must be birthed
and grow to maturity. To deny and thwart the unfolding of that
nature, in any person, is to declare war against an identity that

David in Psalm 139 implied is part of God's eternal plan. The DNA must assume its eventual place in the unfolding kingdom of God. Anger, in these terms, is an understandable expression of humankind.

The wise mentor can turn the mentoree's anger to a good end. Remind the mentoree that the purpose and goal are of God, and that with God's grace, the mentoree is able to complete the task. Anger in the hands of a skilled mentor is a tool that can turn an otherwise weakening mentoree into a person with new resolve.

Paul's precept on anger is noteworthy. "Do not let the sun set on your anger." "Be angry and sin not." Knowing Paul, we understand first that he is quick to recognize and then endorse veiled anger. Second, he cautions about its destructive potential. Paul was a man of intense purpose. Anger was a frequent companion. The Gentiles were destined to hear the gospel, and time was short. Anger at the appropriate time was a motivating force. The commission was from God; the fuel to carry it out often required that he drive himself. In Philippians 4, Paul rejected anything of his past that would hinder him, and he pressed on for the high calling of God in his life. On another occasion, he rejected John Mark, considering him a hindrance to a missionary journey, and he so disagreed with Barnabas over the John Mark issue that he and Barnabas parted company. The skilled mentor will counsel on the best direction anger should take.

The wise mentor will know when the mentoree has to pull back and restrict his or her use of anger. Three times appealing to God to remove the thorn in his flesh brought Paul to anger's line in the sand, but anger had its limits and he committed himself to accept God's sentence on his body. The mentor realizes the thorn in the flesh can also be a badge of identity and part of God's plan. The Romans 7 discourse on Paul's inability to do what he wanted to do and the inability to stop what was wrong led to the exclamation: "Who will remove this civil war within me?" He comes again to the point of anger, and says in Romans 8:1 (parenthetically): "I recognize, despite my inability to shake this thing, I will not be condemned because of it."

Panic

Panic goes beyond fear and is the random and uncoordinated physical or mental flight to avoid the source of fear. Panic is the alternative to anger. It is dread and terror and flees the course, leaving vision and purpose behind. By the time panic takes hold, the mentoree is beyond continuing the journey. Panic is senseless abandonment from the journey. In the midst of the attack, Israel feared, and every man scattered to his own house. Panic is a sign for the mentor to pause from the pursuit of goals and to reassess why the mentoree is in a mentoring relationship.

God, nevertheless, can use panic for His own purposes. The first-century pogroms drove the newly converted Christians to the catacombs and to the hinterland of the then-known world. Randomly fleeing in fear and panic, they scattered to every corner. Terrified, crouching in dark caves over small fires, they prayed, praised, and waited, and they mingled with strange people in strange lands. By the end of the first century, the gospel had spread to all peoples. Panic in the hands of a skillful God turns to eternal purposes.

At the time I was writing this section, I received a call from a mentoree in her mid-thirties who was aggressively pursuing her purposes in God. More than anything, she wanted to establish a close relationship with her Father—the most noble of pursuits. She was successful in sales, single, and had discretionary time to choose from a variety of church-based activities. Overtures from others in the church, however, distracted her; their desire was to get her involved in "their" activities. Distraction had followed its course: anxiety because of the distraction, fear she may lose the preeminent goal in her mind, and, now, anger toward her distracters. It was panic, however, that best described the emotion of her phone call. I have learned a lesson from these kinds of events. Someone cannot easily go from panic back to the beginning; mentors take them from the panic back to the fear, then to the anxiety, and finally back to the distraction and its source. Within thirty minutes, she experienced relief, and we prescribed a new course of action that renewed her hope.

Relief and Renewed Hope

Relief and hope are closely related, and one must distinguish between them. Both occur under similar circumstances, specifically when the obstacles to our progress—distraction, anxiety, fear, and anger—have disappeared.

The first emotional response to having overcome is relief. This is the emotion of "pressure-removed," "breathing easily again," "obstacle gone," or "distraction no more." Scripture defines relief as rest from a condition of endurance and suffering and (less intense) a decrease of anxiety or a rest from persecutions (2 Cor. 2:13; 7:5; 2 Thess. 1:7). How many times, when you have been under the gun for a prolonged period and then the pressure disappears, have you sighed? Your shoulders relaxed, and a faint smile returned.

Relief is a disarming and deceptive substitute for the "hope that does not fail," and the two are often confused to our detriment. Relief is no more than what Scripture says it is: pressure removed. Hope, on the other hand, is the emotion of strength renewed and once again knowing that all the effort to overcome proved worthwhile. *Hope is the emotion* Hope increases with every victory. That is why I *of strength renewed.* have referred to it in chapter 5 as "habit strength." Habit strength does not result from relief! Hope is a favorable and confident expectation when endurance is on trial (1 Thess. 1:3). Hope based on habit strength is an anchor in the storm (Heb. 6:18–19) and a purifying power (1 John 3:3).

Relief is a momentary reprieve, a daydream, in the storms of life and little else. It can precede the return of hope, but it is not hope. The danger comes when we are so relieved by the removal of some type of persecution, deprivation, or disability that we ascribe value to the mere absence of pressure. Christians can be so relieved that a season of suffering is over that they think they are praising God but they are really just welcoming relief. The prior sentence bears a second reading. Relief is deceptive. "Well, that's over," the mentoree exclaims, "and I am out of here; I won't go that route again for anything or anybody. I'm through." Despite the mentor's counsel, the mentoree flees the scene. We confuse relief with hope and settle for the impression of returning hope rather than hope itself. Without hope, habit strength is lacking and the journey ceases.

The mentor must recognize this insidious counterfeit for hope. In a day of quick answers, acupuncture without cure, narcotic reprieve without excision of the tumor, and bad theology that promises more than it can deliver, the mentoree may fall

prey to what a young pastor once counseled to one of his twenty
year olds: "You have borne more than your share of discomfort.
You have paid your dues. Now, get away from the pressure and do
your thing." The counsel provided relief, but it also encouraged
the mentoree to leave the field of action and cease pursuit of her
earlier purposes in God.

Depression or Despair

We mentors are sentries along the road of difficulty the
mentoree travels. If we fall asleep while on watch, the mentoree,
in the midst of difficulties, may slip off the road into a valley of
despair or depression. Depression is the emotion of completely
being without a way and being at a loss without resource (2 Cor. 1:8;
Ps. 88:15). Many are the believers who in the midst of these
emotions cease from hoping for anything again (Col. 3:21).

The wisest of mentors also realize there are times when
mentoree's depression can be a blessing in disguise, as painful as
it may be. Even though the source of our purpose is in God, it still
is possible that both the purpose and the journey can take precedence over the Purpose Giver and our delight in Him. The
thought is not as bizarre as it may seem. Mentorees may lose
perspective and balance and charge ahead, getting off track and
moving independently of the mentor's assignments. The familiar
sequence reappears: distraction, anxiety, fear, anger, and the loss
of hope that translates into depression.

Depression can be caused by correction received because
of youthful or otherwise immature indiscretion. Some writers
think Joseph of the Genesis narrative experienced considerable
depression when his brothers (justifiably, from a human standpoint) threw him into the pit and later sold him to traveling
Egyptians. The pit is a place where one can be still and listen, and
as the occasion merits, repent. The wisest of mentors will sometimes allow it without offering quick fixes. The mentor offers his
or her own seasoned shoulders on which the mentoree can lean
and regain balance. These are not some pabulum or antidepres-
sant, however. "In depression," the mentor assures, "busyness is
brought to a halt, and you can listen and hear a clearer voice than
on the streets of commerce, in the halls of learning, or from the
sanctuary of ministry." Wise is the mentor who carefully guides

the mentoree during such times. A frequent piece of counsel is to slow down, re-center on God, and pull back from being so busy in the affairs of your own making.

CONCLUSION

What lessons have we learned from our study of the emotions? First, we cannot be surprised at the emotions we hear expressed by our mentorees. Second, they can be poor representatives of reality and tied imperfectly to morals, as we quoted Aaron Ben- Ze'ev earlier. Third, not all that our senses perceive will necessarily translate into corresponding emotions. We sense, nevertheless, that they lie somewhere in between what we mentally resolve to do and what we actually do.

Christians are just as susceptible to respond emotionally to environmental challenges as anyone else. I would be concerned if they did not, inasmuch as emotions, in their generic sense, are as much a part of God's creation of man as other attributes. Emotions provide (although imperfectly) indications of where we are in our journey to live out our purposes. They are fellow travelers for all goal-seeking behavior. Christians do, however, differ from unbelievers by having additional resources: the Scriptures, prayer and fasting, the Holy Spirit, the fellowship of believers, and the mentor's encouragement to make use of them.

POSTSCRIPT ON FIGURE 1

A portion of figure 1 has gone unattended in the foregoing discussion. I purposefully did not address the emotions that follow wrath—bitterness, resentment, and unforgiveness. Nor did I include much on the mentoree's need for confession, repentance, and restoration. The reason for this was that by the time mentorees demonstrate wrath and follow that with the "terrible trilogy," they disqualify themselves from the mentoring relationship.

Scripture has much to say about endurance, persistence, overcoming to the end, suffering, and bearing up under discipline and hardship. Hebrews 12:3–17 is notable for the comprehensive way

it addresses what we have been discussing, and all of these challenges flow from the heart of a Father filled with *agape*. There is
the suffering of discipline, such as the discipline associated with
concurrent desocialization and resocialization, and the mentor
does well to guide the mentoree through the social, spiritual,
physical, and psychological obstacle courses that seem ever
present.

Esau, who resisted the challenges of the Father, developed a
root of bitterness and consequently lost his inheritance, so much
so that confession, repentance, and restoration eluded him. What
then is the responsibility of the mentor, whose mentorees have
succumbed to the negative syndrome signified in figure 1's lower
left corner? They wisely use the illustration of Hebrews 12. Here
is the story of a loving Father in whose hands are children whom
He disciplines in order to bring them to maturity and to share
His holiness. Is it not amazing that the God who gives purpose
borne of His love also provides the discipline to bring purpose to
perfection? Those early Christians who heard or read about the
story of Esau in this text needed to know about him, and the
mentor, likewise, tells this story with hope in its promise of
restoration.

P A R T 2

SPECIAL APPLICATIONS TO
LEADERSHIP AND THE MARKETPLACE

CHAPTER SEVEN

Mentoring Future Leaders

THE DIVERSITY OF LEADERSHIP GIFTS MAKES THEM SUFFICIENT TO MEET THE VARIED NEEDS OF THE CHURCH AND ORGANIZATIONS IN THE MARKETPLACE. MENTORS HAVE A GREAT RESPONSIBILITY IN BEING sensitive to how the mentoree's style of leadership fits into the organization.

Three reasons, internal and external to an organization, call for the assessment of mentorees on a regular basis in order to determine how best to mentor them.

First, leadership has grown in importance as the complexity of church policy, staffing, and operations has increased and affected how the church conducts its business. Second, the church is no longer an isolated unobserved island of disinterest to the world around it. Public policies and economic, social, and political forces surround, challenge, and somewhat control how the church is organized. Third, the institutional church, to the extent it desires to be an agent of change in society, will have to develop leaders and through them impact the secular arena.

Its public presence makes clear the church can no longer be content as a neutral observer in a rapidly changing and volatile society without producing capable leadership for both itself and public areas. This does not imply the institutional church must assume an activist posture in the community, although many churches do. Rather, it can produce leaders who enter secular society and make an impact on it. For this to happen, though, leaders must have an extra-local perspective. The two are in reciprocal relationship; the keener the extra-local perspective, the more necessary it will be for the church to develop leaders from within itself. The more new leaders are poured into the community, the more they will return with reports advocating the value of producing new leaders.

Churches need vision and leaders, and without both they will deteriorate and be no more. In George Barna's findings, less than 10 percent of senior pastors, when given a definition of leadership, were able to articulate what they believe God's vision is for the church; only 5 percent say they have the gift of leadership and that they spent less than 16 percent of their time on leadership responsibilities.[1]

It is unreasonable to assume in the absence of leaders that "God will take care of us." God always has accomplished His purposes through leaders, so the question is not *if* there should be leaders. The critical questions are how should mentorees be recognized for their leadership potential? How are they to be trained? And how are they to be mobilized, whether as adjuncts to the pastoral staff or in their respective places of business?

A brief disclaimer is in order. This chapter does not present a detailed plan for leadership development in religious settings, a topic that has received much attention elsewhere. My desire is to show how leadership is of interest to the mentoring program.

LEADERSHIP IN THE BIBLE

The New Testament refers to leaders as those who lead, rule, or guide a church (Heb. 13:7, 14; Rom. 12:8); umpire, arbitrate, and decide issues (Col. 3:15); govern and, like a ship's pilot, steer or show direction (1 Cor. 12:28); and rule as an elder in a home or family (Gal. 4:2; 1 Tim. 3:4, 12; 5:17). Christ is the Shepherd of a flock (Rev. 12:5; 19:15), and the term shepherd is used to describe elders.

The Old Testament elder seems to be the only functional role carried over to the New Testament church without, in the process, undergoing major change. There seems to be no level of human authority in the church mentioned in the New Testament that is higher than the elder. To have been an elder in the primitive church did not mandate that one also had to be one of the "fivefold ministers"—apostle, prophet, evangelist, pastor, or teacher (Eph. 4:11–13). However, to have been any one of these ministers presumes each first had to meet the standards required of an elder. A pastor would not reasonably have been allowed to minister in the church had he not first met the requirements for being an elder—having his own house in order, receiving favor in the community, living a balanced and noble life, and being free from control of wine.

Churches need vision and leaders, and without both they will deteriorate and be no more.

The classic references to leadership being a gift of God are found in 1 Corinthians 12:8 and Romans 12:8. Other references indicate that every church had to have elders.[2] The gifts of 1 Corinthians 12 are parceled out discriminately by God, are deployed in different combinations on an as-needed basis, and are for the edification of church members. All gifts, inclusive of the varieties of leadership, are necessary for a church to function fully.

The Bible implies different types of leadership. The idea of the generic one-size-fits-all leader is rare. Moses was the visionary leader of Israel, but his father-in-law, Jethro, had management leadership qualities and at the right moment came to Moses' rescue. Moses' presumptive murder of the Egyptian guard and the impetuous second strike of the rock were indicative of the darker side of visionary leaders, as I show below. God allowed Moses to see the Promised Land from a high mountain, but He did not permit him to enter, further indicating that the visionary leader has a time and a place and, at some point, may no longer be useful. (Ralph Mattson also makes this point, and I will reference him in a later section.)

Bezalel was the expert leader in design and trades chosen to build the tabernacle in the wilderness. He also had management talents, as he was the overseer of all the other craftsmen, but there is no mention that he had any sense of the vision of the tabernacle. Nehemiah was most definitely a management leader chosen by God to rebuild the Jerusalem wall. Joshua distinguished himself first as a management leader of the army and second as a visionary leader with management capabilities in the settlement of Canaan. Some have observed that only Jesus possessed all the gifts of the Holy Spirit, functioned in all of the ministries of Ephesians 4, and excelled across the four types of leadership mentioned in the next section—visionary, expert, operations, and team builder. His vision was the kingdom of God. He intuitively and precisely laid out a plan He was able to accomplish in three years; He showed expertise in developing a missionary strategy for proclaiming the gospel, and for three years He excelled in developing a highly effective team capable of carrying on in His absence.

Some have said that the mentoring program is the best way to train leaders for the church. The mentor knows there are different leadership types. Mentorees are happier when they know that they will be encouraged in terms of what God has made them to be, and not trained or assigned a position likened to the proverbial square peg forced into a round hole.

CURRENT LEADERSHIP PATTERNS

Seventy percent of pastors surveyed by Barna feel their greatest skills are preaching and teaching; these are the ones they like best, and only an exceptional pastor has both teaching and leadership skills. The evidence supports that most senior pastors are not leaders in the sense of gifting, since only 5 percent say this about themselves, although all hold leadership positions. Another 15 percent consider themselves as having the gifts of administration or management. Every student of leadership agrees, however, that management and leadership are quite different abilities and not transferable from one situation to another.[3]

Steven Covey, for one, describes the difference as follows: "Management is a bottom line focus: How can I best accomplish certain things? Leadership deals with the top line: What are the things I want to accomplish? In the words of Peter Drucker and Warren Bennis, 'Management is doing things right; leadership is doing the right things.' Management is efficiency in climbing the ladder of success; leadership determines whether the ladder is leaning against the right wall."[4]

Influence Versus Leadership

By transmitting information, pastors and teachers change how people think, stir emotions, and give direction. These are the products of what we call *influence*. Influence, however, does not satisfy the demands of leadership. Leadership sets goals, prescribes a plan, and leads others toward goals. Leadership has a permanency to it that influence does not. This is exemplified by the myriad radio and television performers who influence people's ideas but do not assist them in acting on those ideas. Leadership picks up where influence ends.

Early Indications of Leadership

There are eight indicators of future leadership.[5] Mark, a young man of my acquaintance, knew from the time he was in his mid-teens he was going to be a leader, and he is a good example of the evidence of these in his life. Four successful businessmen in Mark's church shared mentoring responsibilities to help him develop into the leader he is today. We use the same indicators to evaluate our mentorees.

- Leaders have an awareness of the calling of God, based on repeated opportunities to lead and feeling comfortable with them.
- Leaders have a natural inclination to lead others, and others are comfortable with their leadership, even when both are younger.
- Leaders are future-oriented, strategically working out solutions to the big picture, which, in some instances, they themselves create.
- Leaders have a posture and presentation of self that communicates leadership to others. Eye contact, handshake, gait, and tone of voice—all communicate: "I am leader material."
- Leaders naturally gravitate to other leaders, even in their growing-up years. There is a compatriot kinship among emerging leaders.
- Leaders draw to themselves those who defer to the leader; deference is "payment" given in exchange for security and guidance received during times of uncertainty and waning motivation.
- Leaders possess and communicate an inner strength. Timidity is not their name; the future is neither a stranger nor a threat.
- Leaders recognize their gift and the signs of emerging calling and purpose in God. They are at home with themselves.

THE MODELS OF LEADERSHIP

We compare two models of leadership. George Barna and Ralph Mattson share one; Burt Nanus represents a more traditional perspective. Mentors benefit from knowing the differences between these and their implications for the mentoring program.

Nanus's Model

Leaders vary in terms of function, according to Nanus. His idea of the *visionary leader* encompasses four different functions relative to the demands placed on the organization. The functions distribute along two axes: the internal versus external environment axis and the present versus the future axis.[6] Figure 2 depicts the four functions.

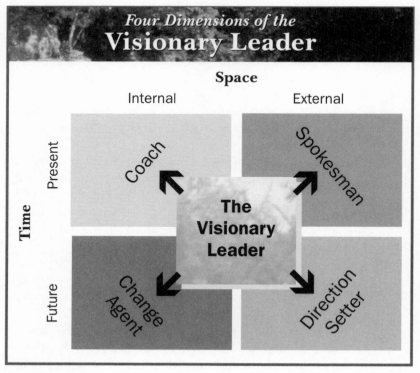

Figure 2

Relative to the organization's internal environment, the leader is the "coach" when acting in the present and is the "change agent" when acting in terms of the future. Relative to the external environment, the leader is the "spokesman" when acting in the present and the "direction setter" when acting in terms of the future. This model assumes the "visionary leader" is capable of performing equally well according to any demand placed on him or her. The model may have had greater utility for an era when it was thought that all functions resided in a single person. Then, the "visionary leader" would have been similar to the monolithic type who is all things to all people. The model's significance for mentors, however, is its identification of leadership functions, which arise relative to environmental demands.

Barna's Model

Barna summarizes a growing trend that leadership gifts come in different packages, and each type of leader has qualities capable of accommodating varying organizational needs. Barna's leadership types do not differ greatly from Nanus's functional differences. For Barna, the functional differences belong to different types of leaders.

There is an element in Barna's model that resembles the body of Christ with functional differences jointly fitted together. First, there is a division of labor among several leadership types. Authority is delegated to a larger number of people. This leads to greater interdependence among the many, rather than dependence on the few, and greater opportunity for individual creativity. Second, since leaders appear more evenly distributed, the organization is "flatter" rather than hierarchical in shape. In a word, the Nanus model would be more at home in the church with a hierarchical structure having a strong person at the head. Barna envisions a church in which multiple leaders fulfill their duties relative to the several missions of the church, some internal or pietistic in nature; others more external or activist in nature.

Each of the model's four types has strengths and weaknesses, thus making interdependence, coordination, synergy, and humility mandatory.[7]

The dominant (or visionary) leader

This leader focuses on vision, capitalizes on ideas, and is strong as the value-driven visionary. However, he or she must also exercise caution regarding his or her reluctance to compromise and the tendency to be impatient and authoritarian.

The strategic (or expert) leader

This leader's strength is in the ability to accumulate the right kind of information with which to analyze every situation. He or she is strong on wisdom, synthesis, reflection, and preparation, and here has no peer. However, despite these strengths, this leader often lacks people skills, is overly perfectionist, and tends to keep feelings inside.

The team-building leader

The team-building leader is the convivial human relations guru, capable of mobilizing others using communication skills and interpersonal strengths such as tact, enthusiasm, and optimism. This leader also has a negative side, particularly when he or she becomes too emotional, is weak in organizational skills, and is less capable of addressing the more global demands put on the organization.

The operations (or management) leader

Here is the consummate manager, architect, and overseer of the formal structure of the organization, devoted to matters of process, accuracy, and efficiency. Because of these strengths, this leader is often insensitive to the need to make exceptions, is not demonstrative, and is overly cautious. For this leader, the goal is the organization or the system, which has more beauty than even the final goal.

The fully equipped church, notes Barna, will have all four types of leaders. If, perchance, only two are available, they preferably will be the dominant and strategic types. These unite readily into a team capable of providing the expert information in which the vision is articulated. Early in their relationship, easily discerned problems or issues will become evident. These leaders can then search for, recruit, and arrange for the training of the other two types of leader. Ideally, the mentors will search throughout the congregation for others who can fill the positions of team and operations leaders.

Mattson's Observations

Ralph Mattson is a Fortune 500 leadership management consultant. He has served many churches and is versed on the scriptural principles of leadership.[8] His model is not significantly different from the one presented by Barna. His value for our discussion, however, lies with several observations about leadership.

First, he is dogmatic on the point that leadership is as distinct a gift as teaching, preaching, counseling, management, and others. All gifts God provides contribute to the synchronized competent administration of the church in the times in which we live (Eph. 1:7–10). One of his observations anticipates the role mentoring could have for the church in leadership development.

> The church sits on top of the largest inactive human resource in the world. Considering the nature of the church's mission, that is a disaster for the world. It isn't that church leaders have not been made aware of the critical need for equipping the saints to do the work of the ministry. . . . The basic problem is that, for the most part, pastors cannot do what is required. There are two reasons for this. One is that there is an inordinate number of controlling pastors . . . through whom every decision must pass. . . . By this action, they . . . present themselves as examples of leaders who believe they possess all the gifts. . . . Such control alienates all those . . . who have careers based on those specialties and who could supply superior contributions in each. . . . The second reason the laity are not in the action is because it requires management gifts to involve people. People need to be recruited and managed appropriately. Pastors are rarely gifted or equipped to . . . do this, nor should they. . . . [Managers] are defined as individuals who have the gifts to work through people to get results. We know managing is a set of gifts that God created because no one else can design human gifts.[9]

A second of Mattson's observations is that no other organization provides more opportunities for motivational leaders as the church. This increases as contemporary churches move from supportive or reaffirming roles in the society-at-large to highly visible leadership. There is danger, nevertheless, of giving too much authority to highly motivating visible leaders. Their tendency, echoing Barna's cautions concerning visionary leaders, is to convert congregations to audiences and distort ministries so they become out-of-balanced crusades. The dominant leader fixes on visions and is happiest when creating them and challenging congregations to pursue them. Out of control, this leader will exhaust a congregation by inciting a move from vision to vision without the balance of managing leaders who assure the stability and longevity of the organization's missions.

Mentors know that mentorees of middle or older years may not be welcome in a church with a strong visionary leader, simply because delegation of authority is rare in these organizations. On occasion, we have referred some of our best mentorees to ministries other than their home church. This is no reason to cease identifying and providing training for upcoming team building, strategic, or operations leaders. The time will come when there is a need for them elsewhere.

LEADERSHIP DEVELOPMENT AND DEPLOYMENT

The process we use for leadership development and deployment involves the following tasks.

- Task 1: The new mentoree completes a questionnaire, which requires a response to the eight leadership indicators cited above. These provide information on one's potential for leading others.
- Task 2: We ask what actual leadership experiences the new mentoree has had in the past. The mentoree is encouraged to answer in detail, drawing from a wide range of experiences.
- Task 3: We compare the information in response to Task 2 with the responses to Task 1. If experience matches potential, we move on to determining a person's leadership style.
- Task 4: We use either the Barna or Mattson models, or some combination, to derive a leadership style for the mentoree.

The new mentoree frequently is not prepared to enter or begin training for a leadership role and must await the completion of more basic tasks. Our desire always is to have the mentoree eventually express insights on personal calling and purpose, which I describe in chapter 4. Our experience has been that mentorees first give priority to whatever "maintenance needs" they may have, and we always oblige them. Some want instruction on how to develop a deeper prayer life, to better communicate with others, to more effectively interpret Scripture, to search for a job, to develop a budget, to conduct a biblical courtship, to be a better father or husband, and a host of others. Success in any of these invariably raises a mentoree's hope that he or she can complete other tasks. We prefer starting the mentoring relationship with a series of smaller tasks, in order to assure success. This not only builds hope. It also increases the mentoree's trust in the mentor and gives the mentor greater opportunity to learn more about the mentoree.

Leadership Training

Every organization has a number of people with various skills available to assist in the mentoring process on an as-needed basis. One of the more valuable assets of any mentoring program coordinator is a big Rolodex. The Rolodex is a takeoff of the information and referral services many organizations use for referring clients to partner organizations for specialized services. In churches, this "Rolodex" contains the body of Christ, and we develop a list of members with specialized skills who have agreed to assist us whenever their skills are in need. In other words, no mentor expects to have all the skills required by the mentoree. One member had recently purchased an accounting firm and he wanted mentoring on how to market his services and how to set up an office practice. In his own church, there was a certified public accountant we enlisted for his expertise in marketing accounting services. Another CPA belonging to a different church had many years experience in office practice management, and she agreed to provide counsel for the mentoree. The mentor with the primary responsibility monitored the progress of each referral until there were satisfactory results.

Our Rolodex also includes a variety of leaders each having one of the leadership styles listed by Barna. These have agreed to serve as consultants to our mentorees who are ready to further develop their skills. We arrange a joint meeting between the lead mentor, the consultant, and the

No mentor expects to have all the skills required by the mentoree.

mentoree. We explain the nature of the relationship, what we expect of the consultant and mentoree, and provide duplicate management forms for their use. They agree on specific goals that the mentoree is to pursue, the tasks that are necessary to reach them, and target dates for task completion. With completion of each task, the leader enters progress comments on the management form. The mentor will monitor the training process and be available when requested by either the consultant or the mentoree.

Leadership Deployment

Deployment occurs at two levels. Mentorees who have been in an apprentice relationship with leaders return to their present positions more skilled than before. Some remain as assistants to the leaders who apprenticed them.

The second group consists of those enrolled in our mentor training programs, who come from many different positions. Some are church-based and others have salaried or professional positions in the marketplace. All who have taken the mentor training program, following completion, report on how the program has helped them in their positions of leadership.

A few of the graduates and their benefits from the programs are listed here. A registered nurse applied principles in her supervisory role to other nurses on a hospital oncology unit. An assistant human relations manager returned to work at a national corporation more capable in negotiating employee complaints. An executive secretary learned new skills on how to "protect" her boss from irate clients. A fifth-grade Sunday school teacher returned to her class more skilled in how to apply love in a constructive manner. Several home group leaders began to mentor members of their home groups and maintained contact with their program coordinator for ongoing coaching. An account manager for a national talent agency applied the principles of the next chapter, and remained in his place of work more energized, convinced that God had a place for him in the marketplace. An accounts payable manager was more proactive in directing her son's therapy team. A psychiatrist was more convinced that God had a special role for him to play among his colleagues, and he returned to his place of work more emboldened for the gospel. A salesman's greatest benefit from mentor training was the more proactive role he assumed as a godly husband and leader in his home. An assistant in a financial counseling firm returned to her job so assured that she was where God had placed her and of the testimony she was to declare, that at a later date the owner of the firm reported in a positive note that she had become the firm's "conscience." The professor husband of one of our graduates asked what we had done to change his wife. He observed that she was more directive of others whom she was mentoring than he had ever seen her and said: "Whatever you're doing, don't stop; she's remarkable." There are many reports such as these about mentors who had a leadership impact in their places of work, in the church, and in their homes.

C H A P T E R   E I G H T

Mentoring for the Marketplace

THE MARKETPLACE IS A PLACE OF CONTESTED PHILOSOPHIES AND
CHALLENGED LOYALTIES. CHURCH MEMBERS WILL FIND THEY CAN
INFLUENCE THE WORLD WITH A MESSAGE OF REDEMPTION AND
restoration that derives from the application of kingdom principles to the marketplace. Mentors, who themselves have lived on
the edge, can impart these principles to their mentorees.

Jesus masterfully taught the parables through metaphor and
simile. He communicated deep spiritual truths in terms understood by people at all levels. He had no equal to His knowledge of
history and culture. He addressed people not in the terms of high
theology and the dissected intricacies of doctrine but in the
language of the street. The kingdom was like a field, a net, a
mustard seed, a pearl of great price, and a lost coin.

He dealt in spiritual verities, yet He was of the natural world,
and no topic or experience of secular life escaped use in His parables and relationships. His experience extended to the smell and
slime of the fish market and the leathery-tough hands of the
plowman. He knew the dust from sanding a piece of furniture and
the chaff that filled the eyes of the winnower. He was sensitive to
the hate imposed on the tax collector and the claim Caesar
placed on the coin. He painfully winced in concert with the final
shudder and gasp of the criminal impaled to a Roman cross. He
understood, while rejecting, the rage of those who screamed
"adulteress," but recognized the value of pure nard poured on his
feet by a redeemed harlot. He knew what it took to preserve
vintage wine. He knew the intricacies of herding sheep and

thrusting a stiletto into a ram's stomach distended by gas produced by green grass. He knew how to confront the hypocrites, acknowledged the authority of a centurion, did not yield to unclean spirits and graveyard demoniacs, and felt mercy for those whom scurrying crowds called "unclean."

Jesus never met a stranger. No person or the place he or she came from was strange to Him. He was never off guard because of ignorance of the kind of work a person did and the worldly environment from which he or she came. This kind of familiarity with the marketplace is the model all dedicated mentors need to bring to maturity the calling and purposes of entrepreneurs, business executives, laborers, professionals, and salaried employees. This same familiarity is of inestimable worth when used to teach seminarians and those recently graduated from seminaries.

LEARNING BY EXPERIENCE

My young pastor had known me for half a dozen years and finally got around to asking me how I made a living. He asked if he could follow me to my place of work. I appreciated the inquiry inasmuch as I had already been the senior elder in his church for several years. At the time, I had a tension-provoking job as a project review officer. Once a month I conducted public hearings where my duties often made me the target of high-ranking CEOs, who frequently criticized and attacked (with derision, flushed faces, and bulging carotid arteries) my decisions regarding their pet projects. The day my pastor accompanied me was one of those days. From the back of the room, he listened to my attackers for eight hours. That evening, he had only one thing to say, "I will never preach the same again; I had no idea this is what could happen to my people." C. S. Lewis once wrote:

> We must learn the language of our audience. Moreover, let me
> say . . . it is no use laying down *a priori* what the "plain man"
> does or does not understand. You have to find out by experience
> . . . [and] . . . translate every bit of your theology into the
> vernacular. This is very troublesome . . . but it is essential. It is
> also of the greatest service to your own thought . . . [for] . . . if
> you cannot translate your own thoughts into uneducated

language, then your thoughts are confused. Power to translate
is the test of having really understood your own meaning.[1]

Jesus' familiarity with the marketplace, by example alone,
demands a proactive effort by mentors to improve the ability of
those who labor in the secular arena to understand and apply
biblical truth to the workplace. The goal is to equip men and
women with a kingdom perspective and for them to proclaim it
by example and word in the secular arena! Mentors are not
exempt from knowing the culture of the marketplace. They have
learned the language through having been there. Their experience is God's deposit in them, and that is one reason the Father
has put into their hearts a desire to mentor.

From time to time, I had mentored a friend who was a banker.
He was familiar with the biblical principles of finance and stewardship and told how people would come to him for a loan. Many
of his clients qualified for a loan. My friend learned some of these
could get along without having to borrow, so he counseled them
about debt and personal and corporate stewardship. They happily
left with a new financial plan for their businesses without having
to borrow. That was a kingdom approach to
handling debt.

Over the years, businessmen and professionals
said they would welcome a set of biblical principles
for use in their places of work, and they knew non-
Christians who were seeking the same thing. Some
Christian organizations have helped meet these
kinds of needs, and some excellent books are available. The institutional church has two reasons to
provide this kind of service through its mentoring
program. First, it has the responsibility to prepare
its members to be kingdom people in the marketplace. Second, it needs to demonstrate to its
members that church leaders recognize the kind
of challenges they face daily.

We have taught the principles in this chapter
to many groups of mentors-in-training. We assign
the materials several weeks before discussing
them in class. One of our trainees, who held a responsible job in
a music industry booking agency, had tried several times to

*Jesus' familiarity
with the market-
place, by example
alone, demands a
proactive effort by
mentors to improve
the ability of those
who labor in the
secular arena to
understand and
apply biblical truth
to the workplace.*

contact me, leaving a message that there was something important to discuss and that it may involve leaving his present place of employment. At the time he called, he had these materials for a week. We did not, however, make contact until the evening of the next class.

He rushed in, excited, and shouted: "I read the material, and it's worth the whole course. It has transformed my thinking about working where I am. I've decided to stay put and be a kingdom man in the marketplace." Since making that decision, this new mentor has co-mentored with me. He reports that numerous changes have taken place in his business that reflect God's blessings because "the kingdom has come."

A BIBLICAL UNDERSTANDING OF THE MARKETPLACE

A biblical understanding of the marketplace is necessary if mentors are to prepare people to "occupy until He comes." The church is always responsible for the community wherever the church exists. It is not the church-in-exile, nor is it merely buildings that serve as modern-day alternatives to first-century catacombs.

The balance between being pietistic and socially active, as I explained in chapter 2, requires the church to completely be a kingdom church. Half a biscuit does not count. The social gospel is always a prophetic message when it witnesses to the "finger of God" intruding on the affairs of man, and it often conveys a contrary way of doing things. It brings truth, repentance, and healing to the community through its pastors, its volunteer ministers, and through its members, the majority of whom move into the nooks and crannies of every office, shop, classroom, hospital, and factory, as well as into the citadels of government and finance. Being involved in the health-care industry for over three decades, I am intimately acquainted with many of the ways the sometimes obtrusive and sometimes invisible "finger of God" has worked throughout that complex system of hospitals, physicians' offices, nursing homes, and private and public agencies. I have seen the kingdom of God in the marketplace.

Seven principles give the mentor a way to prepare the mentoree for work. Following each principle I suggest how the mentor can relate it to a mentoree's work situation.

God Owns and Holds Legal Title to the Marketplace

The beginning of the biblical record is direct and non-debatable: "In the beginning God . . ." God was before all and created all, and He sustains all that He created. As Creator, He owns and holds legal claim to all things. Jesus' sovereignty is two-fold.

Sovereignty means all-inclusive lordship

The idea of God's sovereignty is foreign to most ears and unimaginable in terms of real life, except for the ability of the mentor to give examples (soon to be discussed). Sovereigns rule totally and all-inclusively. God is the Sovereign over nations, and He has established their boundaries and seasons. He also is Lord over those who do not know Him, including heads of transnational corporations and conglomerates that flaunt independence from Him. The same applies to policy makers, at all levels, who are antagonistic toward Him. Our faith tells us He is sovereign over the marketplace, but it is a faith that often has to wait for concrete examples.

The sum of these thoughts is that there is no such thing as "God" unless He is all of these and more. Our limited vocabulary makes it impossible to express the ultimate. When comprehended even casually, however, these truths about God convert the meek among us into men and women who have greater confidence, hope, and boldness.

The creation is purposeful

The message of chapter 4 was that there is purpose for all things—the physical creation, the creation and redemption of man, and the epochs and times.

God's first words to Adam and Eve were that they were to steward over creation and make it productive to meet the ultimate purposes of God. We can discover the principles governing stewardship and productivity, and when we do, the secrets and joys of the creation are unlocked for us

The mentor's counsel

Mentors will draw from their own experience, or from those known to them, examples of God's marketplace sovereignty and how they or acquaintances have purposefully performed in the marketplace to make it productive. Our experience has been that the mentoree's faith builds tremendously when armed with the mentor's "war stories" and exploits. The wise mentor will choose illustrations that are within the mentoree's ability to appreciate. This means to "grade" the account to the mentoree's present level of faith or just beyond it. We often counsel that the Christian in the marketplace must develop the gift of discernment (1 Cor. 12:10), which can protect the Christian from harm or can open doors of opportunity.

Delegated Husbandry

God's first words were ethical, transferring to us the responsibility for sustaining and expanding the creation. Husbandry means to multiply and contribute to fruitfulness throughout the earth. Created in the image of God, humankind has two ways to rule.

Family as microcosm of the kingdom

God rules through the family, whose design and purpose is biological and economic. The husband cares for the wife, and she assists him in his responsibilities for management and productivity. From the beginning until the present, their relationship is one of interdependence.

Working side by side, the husband and wife go beyond mere maintenance of what God has given them. They nurture the creation and make it fruitful for the long term. Their stewardship includes having children, in order to assure future generations of stewards.

The family under God continues as the basic economic unit of stewardship and fruitfulness. In the church, those who are not part of a nuclear family nevertheless have the responsibility of encouraging families to carry out their God-given mandates. Frequently, the mentors we train include both husband and wife, often simultaneously. It is infrequent that the spouse of a mentoree fails to be included at some point in our mentoring.

The synergy of natural and spiritual spheres

Scripture does not separate spiritual truths from natural affairs. Spiritual verities eventually express themselves in behavior;

behavior reflects underlying spiritual principles. Our fellowship with God is spiritual, so husbanding the natural order of things is evidence of our spiritual relationship with God. Stewardship is the process in which heaven and earth come together.

The mentor's counsel

The mentor quotes from marketplace data that when husbands and wives work closely together, the synergy of their efforts exceeds the sums of their individual efforts. Many people call and inquire of the mentoring program and are relieved when they learn that life's purposes are as applicable to the secular marketplace as they are in religious pursuits. We often quote Youth With A Mission (YWAM) founder Loren Cunningham who at two successive mission conferences commented: "The worst lie from the pit of hell is the one saying that ministry is restricted to being a pastor, youth leader, or missionary. Ministry is whatever God tells you to do and you do with all your heart and for Him."

Redemption and Restoration of the Creation

Our ancestors and the generations since have willfully rejected their role as stewards of creation and traded that stewardship for presumed ownership over the creation. Chapter 1 made clear that God, in the spirit of *agape*, gave, but we took control and misused the creation in the spirit of *eros*. Despite our decadence, God did not renege from His initiative, and the mandate to steward remained.

Pride and resistance to work

Hampered by acquisitive ambition and pride, we presumed ownership of and control over the creation in two ways. First, we translated our power into laziness and resistance against God's command to oversee, manage, and be fruitful. Unholy people resist the holiness of work, while holy people take pleasure in doing work and produce joyful and skillful benefits for others who participate in the fruitfulness.

Second, unbelievers enter the marketplace pursuing personal gratification and self-importance. Believers see the marketplace as a place where a forgiven and redeemed people steward God's creation according to God-given gifts and restore it to fruitfulness for kingdom purposes and the benefit of others.

The mentor's counsel

The mentor makes clear the hate *eros* has for *agape* and fore-warns that the wrong motive for marketplace involvement can rob a person of divine purpose. Job descriptions and responsibilities may be the same for believers and unbelievers alike. This is not the issue. Actions always expose the thoughts and motives of the heart. The incarnated Word carried by the believer shines light on the *eros* of the unbeliever; the latter flees the light, conforms to it, or strikes back. One of our trainees reported that her supervisor instructed her to falsify figures on the firm's financial status report. She refused, fully aware her refusal was tantamount to insubordination and could result in termination. Instead, the supervisor withdrew his request, watched her for several months, and eventually promoted her to manage a small work group.

Believers see the marketplace as a place where a forgiven and redeemed people steward God's creation according to God-given gifts and restore it to fruitfulness for kingdom purposes and the benefit of others.

Mentors watch over the souls of mentorees and help negotiate the options available to a kingdom person. Jealously and envy are common in the workplace, as are rumors, slander, gossip, and defamation. Kingdom people who follow the counsel of the mentor will by no means always be welcomed by a non-redeemed crowd, but their desire still is to promote redemption and restoration of the marketplace.

When the mentoree reports problems at work, the mentor first refuses to respond casually. For the mentoree, these are often matters of survival. After examining the facts, the mentor may conclude the mentoree has acted wrongly, in which case he or she corrects and recommends a scriptural prescription (2 Tim. 3:14–16). The mere occurrence of challenges and threats in the marketplace, however, is not evidence that the mentoree is failing in faith or that "God punishes for wrongdoing." Any mentor who has worked many years in the marketplace knows summary judgments are insufficient. The principles appearing throughout this book provide guidance to help the mentoree navigate his or her way through enemy territory and otherwise rough waters. The psalmist graphically describes his own testing on the waters of commerce in Psalm 107:23–30, which reconfirms there is nothing new under the sun.

Those who go down to the sea in ships, Who do business on great waters; They have seen the works of the Lord, And His wonders in the deep. For He spoke and raised up a stormy wind, Which lifted up the waves of the sea. They rose up to the heavens, they went down to the depths; Their soul melted away in *their* misery. They reeled and staggered like a drunken man, And were at their wits' end. Then they cried to the Lord in their trouble, And He brought them out of their distresses. He caused the storm to be still, So that the waves of the sea were hushed. Then they were glad because they were quiet; So He guided them to their desired haven.

Call to Faithfulness and Excellence

God calls us to faithfulness (2 Tim. 2:2). Stewardship requires that excellence march alongside faithfulness. The two are reciprocal in nature. Faithfulness in performance increases our skills, and these in turn lead to excellence of performance. Excellence in performance, then, encourages us to further faithfulness.

Faithfulness in performance

The lessons of faithfulness begin in the family. Parents teach children to be stewards first over small things, usually their own toys, and this grows to include the family, school, church, and finally their God-given places in the marketplace. Many have been the parents who admonished their teenagers: "I want that room so clean it looks like the kingdom of God."

An important evidence of faithfulness is in the use of money. Money makes bartering unnecessary and causes the marketplace to be a more efficient and versatile place to meet one's needs. Money places "value" on time, material goods, and storage—putting aside today for tomorrow's needs. Its faithful use enables us to exercise control, to the extent it depends on us, over the future, and this frees us to respond to God's call on our lives. Faithfulness with money directly ties to living out our purposes in God. Money accumulated through debt rather than surplus rejects the principle of productivity; creates a false and unearned blessing; and represents blessing to and by oneself rather than that given by God.

Money can be stored for times when we do not work (vacation, illness), when we are in retirement (or have slowed in our labors), or when disaster strikes (famine or drought). Accumulated surpluses provide the faithful mentoree a remarkable number of options from which to choose when pursuing his or her purposes in God.

Excellence in performance

God was excellent in His creation, and He expects us to be excellent in the marketplace. We cannot be excellent in all things, but God enables and expects us to be excellent in the service He gives us to do. The principles on the use of money help us understand the relationship between faithfulness and excellence. Excellent work produces a surplus. Faithfulness is the means by which we reduce debt through surplus. Faithfulness and excellence work in tandem to give value to many things that are not in the here and now.

The mentor's counsel

The marketplace is the most public place where the combination of excellence and faithfulness is visible and evaluated by others. To the boss, the two together mean profit for the company, and they are encouraged. To one's peers, however, it often incites jealousy and envy. The mentoree is in between opposing loyalties. The mentor admits that mentorees could avoid the envy of their peers by lessening faithfulness and excellence, but then they would not be faithful employees. On the other hand, the mentor continues, the mentoree could endure envy and thereby satisfy the employer, the company's board of directors, and the shareholders. The marketwise mentor knows how to balance these contrary pressures and teach them to the mentoree.

We cannot be excellent in all things, but God enables and expects us to be excellent in the service He gives us to do.

Biblical Principles for Productivity

God's principles for productivity have never changed, yet history shows that several economic models govern market forces. The Christian confronts these often in the form of conflicting messages. Our concept of productivity began with God's ownership and rule over the marketplace and His delegation to us to steward it using the gifts and resources given to us. There are three paths we can follow to be productive.

The Audience of One

The major force ruling the marketplace is *eros*. It is the self-centered, self-aggrandizing, and humanistic approach to marketplace forces. Socialism and capitalism both express this view in several ways (discussed below). The mentor counsels according to the following logic:

- The Christian is the main vehicle for taking a kingdom message to the marketplace, and
- the standards set for the marketplace originate at the level of public policy; therefore
- the Christian in the marketplace uses God's wisdom to demonstrate the value of God's ways and therefore redeem the marketplace through changes in corporate and public policy.

These ideas encourage and motivate mentorees whom God directs to the marketplace. The shift in recent years from top-heavy authoritarian structures to flatter ones in the marketplace provides more, not fewer, chances for employees to contribute to corporate welfare. Flatter structures open the door for individual creativity borne out of each individual's gifts and talents to reward employers and bring acclaim to Christians. This is the essence of Paul's criterion regarding the qualifications for being an elder: They should be people who receive honor in their work. Therefore, the Christian's influence of corporate and public policy is a goal worthy of pursuit.

The following discussion on socialistic and capitalistic economic models, while superficial, is sufficient to show that at the heart of the philosophy or values of all economic models is an assumed "image of man." The mentor's task is to convey that mentorees carry with them the "image of God," and this is likely to differ from critical aspects of socialism and capitalism.

A socialistic model

Socialism is a system where the state owns or controls the means of production. The government holds title to businesses such as parks, hospitals, schools, and railroads. It controls others in varying degree through taxation (applied to all for-profit corporations), subsidization (to control what is and what is not produced, such as in agriculture), mediation or arbitration of labor and management disputes, anti-trust or anti-monopoly laws, safety regulations, minimum wage, and numerous others. Some non-profit corporations (schools, churches) are subject to controls in terms of what they teach or preach and who is hired.

The inherent assumption in this model is that government is wiser in governing the affairs of life than private individuals are. Few would argue that certain aspects of public life, such as in the area of pubic utilities (highways, electrical grids, metropolitan water systems, and military preparedness) are beyond most private capabilities. Others would argue vehemently that education of children, private investment for retirement (rather than social security), negotiating private contracts between workers and employers, postal services, and others, are within the capabilities of private decision-making.

The Soviet form of totalitarian communism was extreme socialism since the government owned all means of production and used central planning to force compliance through threat of punishment, incarceration, or execution. Karl Marx predicted the West would engage socialism. His predictions in many ways have proven accurate. We have state-owned and/or controlled schools, health care, public utilities, public lands, banking and securities systems, and others. To the extent that the state dictates the rearing or education of children, the unfettered practice of religion, or the contracts between employer and employee are "Marxist" or socialist. Governmental control often results in state-granted job security (e.g., in governmental bureaucracies and public education) at the expense of personal creativity and accountability. Other characteristics of socialism include:

- Public policy and practices encourage covetousness and envy toward those who have been industrious, faithful, and seeking excellence.
- Public policy makes the prosperous feel guilty for succeeding.
- Taxation is a means of leveling wealth, by distributing the surpluses of the more successful to provide for those who do not produce.
- All are equal by ignoring God-given gifts and talents.

The mentor's counsel

The mentor begins by challenging mentorees to consider whether they lay claim to a biblical or a socialistic image of humankind. A socialistic image has the government making otherwise private decisions, and those may run counter to the mentoree's responsibility for a Christian witness. Nowhere in contemporary society is the dichotomy of the two images greater than in parents' biblical responsibility for the education of their children. Whereas private schooling may not be the only option for parents to exercise, we point out that a kingdom approach by parents to public education involves participation in parent/teacher organizations and the development of personal relationships with teachers to assure that non-Christian educators do not influence children contrary to Christian upbringing. (A personal testimony to this is in the notes.[2])

The diversity of opportunity in the American marketplace is such that we know of no set of purposes ordained by God that are limited as to their creativity and productive expression.

The marketplace expression of *eros* under the umbrella of socialistic practices includes policy makers and governmental agents acting in behalf of some dispossessed or disadvantaged group. Rousas Rushdoony has referred to this as the "politics of guilt and pity."[3] In the same vein Marvin Olasky has written of the tragedy of American compassion[4] and Thomas Sowell of the decline, deception, and dogmas of American education.[5] According to Rushdoony, policy makers pity the less fortunate (usually because they envy the more successful and make others feel guilty for indirectly depriving them through the misuse of "excessive" abundance). They pass laws to redistribute wealth through taxation or expropriation of property. Examples of income redistribution include entitlements for health care and food subsidies, subsidization of special industries, and anti-discrimination hiring practices. The Christian response to entitlement, however, is to feed the poor, clothe the naked, house the dispossessed, and care for the widows, widowers, and orphans. Colonel V. Doner captures this in *The Samaritan Strategy*.[6]

A capitalistic model

Capitalism has had an interesting history. The account given of its development by the sociologist Max Weber has value for our discussion. Weber distinguished between "true capitalism" and "false capitalism." True capitalism, he felt, had roots in Calvinism and therefore met some of the biblical criteria for marketplace behavior. True capitalism saw profit as evidence of God's grace upon the elect who then hired additional people who otherwise would remain unemployed. Unemployment kept others from finding their rightful place in God's economy. Therefore, the early capitalist was frugal and industrious, accumulated surpluses, and put others to work. All of these were evidence of proper stewardship over what God had given to man.

Capitalism in America changes when profits become an end rather than a means to a greater end. When profits result in conspicuous consumption, Weber called this false capitalism, which lacked its earlier religious roots.

Capitalism retains certain qualities consistent with a kingdom model—private ownership, accountability, giving, initiative, and effort-generated rewards. When false capitalism is in effect, it possesses four qualities best described by *eros*:

- The pursuit of profit as the end goal
- The use of people to its own ends
- A utilitarian use of people without regard for their God-given calling and purposes
- Pursuit of profit based on greed, exploitation, and unhealthy competition leading to the destruction of God's creation rather than managing and replenishing the earth

The mentor's counsel

The issue is not capitalism, per se, but any expression of it that reflects false capitalism. The mentor's counsel will address any of the four foregoing qualities, relative to the mentoree's options. The mentor may counsel the mentoree to seek employment with a company run according to the kingdom principles found here; to start their own company; or to influence a present employer according to kingdom principles. The appropriate option depends on the mentoree's level of maturity, preparedness to respond to counsel, and God's plan for him or her.

More and more companies are producing socially beneficial products, providing socially redeeming services, and taking employee welfare seriously. Still others invest profits in "social investments," such as inner-city renovation. To again quote John Beckett, " . . . everything is holy if it is surrendered to and in harmony with the Lord. This includes our vocations as long as they are not contrary to His righteous standards." There are, therefore, companies that contribute to the welfare of the families of their employees, by not requiring excessive overtime by family heads, by providing liberal time for maternity leave, and by offering meaningful Employee Assistance Plans. These companies are making an effort to match personal gifts and talents to job requirements.

The pursuit of profit at the expense of societal, corporate, and employee welfare is a danger signal for the marketplace. In the extreme, it destroys the environment, ignores quality control over physical and equipment resources, and endangers employee and consumer safety.

The mentor's use of a personal network of contacts—the matrix of believers within the body of Christ—provides the mentoree viable options for choosing employment options consistent with kingdom principles.

The Principle of Sowing and Reaping

The principle of sowing and reaping addresses how the employee uses surplus or the business owner uses profits. The parable of the sower and the seed is a warning on how to sow wisely. The seed is metaphor for the gifts God gives to each person. The earlier principles of faithfulness and excellence set the stage for the principle of productivity that produces a surplus. The principle of sowing and reaping, on the other hand, governs how surpluses are used.

Management of wealth

Wealth is the accumulation of large amounts of surplus, or profit, gained by the wise use of our gifts and resources. Accumulated surpluses belong to God, just as God gave us gifts that generate surpluses.

The mentor's counsel

Mentors guide in the disposition of wealth. Four ways exist to manage wealth. Wise mentors recommend balance regarding the distribution of surplus in order to preserve its amount as well as earn interest on its investment.

- They counsel on impending events that threaten accumulation—economic downturns, disasters, and policy changes.
- They inform of events or circumstances regarding reallocations of surplus, such as charitable needs, high priority missionary activities, or socially redemptive investments.
- They counsel on the control of desire that consumes wealth carelessly, by recommending saving or investing wealth to make it less accessible. Options include long-term government bonds or Blue Chip mutual funds. Surplus also is less accessible if invested in surplus-equivalents, such as life insurance or long-term health care insurance. Older adults who invest in long-term care insurance for themselves, or older children who purchase it for their parents, protect the assets of two generations.
- They counsel to prepare for realistic yet unpredictable emergencies. Accumulated wealth can be accessible or "liquid" assets. Liquidity is a measure of how quickly the mentoree can access surplus in the event of reversals, such as sudden sickness or disability, fire or flood loss, or a major automobile accident. Liquidity also exists as cash-equivalents—food, medicine, and equipment storage for use in the event of an emergency.

The readiness and ability of the mentoree to respond to the Holy Spirit is the over-riding principle governing the accumulation of wealth and its management. The marketplace provides for our needs and beyond in the form of surpluses. God blesses us and enables us to bless others through accumulated wealth that we invest in others. Investment in others leads to new surpluses in the lives of those we bless.

Free from Work's Control of Our Lives

The seventh principle derives from the seventh day: God rested. The Sabbath is not so much a day of rest from what lies behind as much as it is a preparation for what lies ahead. It is a day of reprieve; a day without work is a testimony that work shall not control a person who is a steward over work and not slave to it. Translated, it means that humankind was to produce in six days whatever was required to live seven days and still provide a surplus to help others or ourselves in times of need

THE ULTIMATE VISION

The ultimate vision for the church, each family, and each person in the marketplace is the same—to bring glory to God and make His glory known throughout the earth.

The Honorable Carlos Davelas, secretary general of the Pan American Union during the 1950s, shared a story from his home country of Brazil. "Brazil is not known as a Christian nation, yet our government and businesses everywhere seek for Christians as employees and particularly those in management, for they bring honesty and honor to the nation and to corporations. Their witness is known everywhere." Brazilian believers took with them into the marketplace a kingdom message.

The quintessential issue is that the mentoring program prepare men and women to take to the marketplace the highest caliber of labor which in the main makes God's glory known among all people.

For over three decades, our three companies provided consulting services nationwide to rural health-care facilities. Wherever our employees went, from hospital to hospital, we customarily sought out the person we assumed God had placed there to provide a Christian witness.

One particularly small hospital located in the Appalachian Mountains was in a state of disarray: the physicians would not cooperate with the administrator, the administrator communicated poorly with nurse supervisors, and employees at the lower echelons were constantly bickering. After a week on site, we had located God's person for that hospital, the supervisor of social services. Betty was as concerned about what was not happening at the hospital as we were. We could not move forward with the services we had contracted to perform.

I called my wife who managed our company's home office, some five hundred miles away, and asked that she call together

her "heavy hitters"—a small group of praying and fasting women we called any time we needed damage control.

In two weeks, Betty saw me and asked what had happened in the hospital. The doctors and administrator were holding meetings and ironing out differences. The nursing staff seemed to have a change of heart and were congenial; other workers were joking, laughing, and slapping each other on the back; the food in the dining hall had gotten better; and the floors were shining like new.

I explained to Betty what had taken place—kingdom people did the kingdom thing, and the finger of God had prevailed. Then I concluded: "This is what you were brought here to do. Our work will be over soon, but you are the kingdom emissary to this place, and you have to continue what we started. You are but one person, but through you God can work in this place." We repeated this everywhere we contracted. If only for a few weeks or a month or two, we would mentor local Christians to their kingdom responsibilities in their piece of the marketplace.

The quintessential issue is that the mentoring program prepare men and women to take to the marketplace the highest caliber of labor which in the main makes God's glory known among all people.

P A R T 3

MANAGING THE MENTOR PROGRAM

CHAPTER NINE

Choosing the Mentoree and the Mentor

CHOOSING AND MATCHING MENTOREES AND MENTORS ARE TWO OF
THE MORE IMPORTANT TASKS IN THE MENTORING ENTERPRISE. IN THIS
CHAPTER, I DISCUSS SELECTION CRITERIA FROM BOTH SECULAR AND
religious literature. I also give attention to the choice of atypical
mentorees and mentors.

CHOOSING THE MENTOREES

Margo Murray's *Beyond the Myths and Magic of Mentoring* is one
of the more authoritative secular books on mentoring, and
several well-known Christian writers refer to its place in the
mentoring literature. Murray identifies self-recruitment, boss
and supervisor, and sponsor recommendations as the three
sources for identifying and enrolling mentorees. In Murray's
experience, sponsors usually know the most about future
mentorees and are less inclined to hold inaccurate stereotypes
about their potential. She distinguishes between the essential
characteristics of high potential candidates and the responsibilities expected of them.[1]

Characteristics

The mentoree is (1) goal oriented, (2) willing to assume responsibility for his or her own growth and development, (3) receptive to
feedback and coaching, (4) actively seeking challenging assignments

135

and greater responsibility, and (5) a person of high impact and low maintenance.

Responsibilities

The mentoree is expected to (1) identify developmental needs and set goals, (2) formulate an action plan to accomplish goals, (3) document the development plan, and (4) maintain regular contact with a program coordinator on progress being made with the mentor. Murray summarizes these responsibilities as "facilitated mentoring," in contrast to "non-facilitated mentoring," which is more indecisive and similar to what I call (but do not recommend) the "fateful chemistry" approach to mentoring.

Christian writers have retained but added to Murray's criteria. I compiled the following list from Bobb Biehl, Charles Simpson, Ted Engstrom, and Howard and William Hendricks, whom I reference in the appendix and bibliography.

- The mentoree has insight into his or her own needs, is goal-oriented, and seeks challenging assignments and greater responsibilities.
- There is early evidence of a sense of purpose, often referred to as vision, mission, or God-given destiny.
- The mentoree has a teachable spirit and puts aside the pride that prevents growth.
- The mentoree demonstrates initiative and is willing to be a doer, not just a hearer of the Word, thereby readily accepting responsibility.
- The mentoree will have open eyes, recognizing that mentors are human and have the responsibility of making the mentoree more dependent on the Lord than on the mentor.
- The mentoree has a servant's heart as it applies to the mentor.
- The mentoree will gradually increase in transparency, as the relationship with the mentor grows; some refer to this as becoming more "like family."
- The mentoree will not be "high maintenance and low impact" and will have the potential for purpose-related leadership.

- The mentoree is willing to be accountable to an agreed-upon agenda for improvement. This includes appointments, assignments, and reaching completion target dates.

In the first interview with the mentoree, the mentor reviews the principles found in chapters 1 and 2, thereby laying the basis for the mentoring relationship. Mentors invite mentorees to ask for clarification on these perspectives and are assured of their willingness to pursue personal growth with these in mind.

We ask all mentorees to list two to three needs they want to address or goals they wish to pursue and reach over the first four to six months of mentoring. In addition, they must write a two-page autobiography of key events in their lives and conclude the autobiography in a manner that includes a restatement of the needs or goals. (A discussion on the autobiography is in chapter 4.) The mentor also writes an autobiography. We use the two autobiographies as a means to match mentor with mentoree.

Recruiting Mentorees: What Experience Has Taught

Four sources of referrals have produced most of the mentorees for our programs.

- Mid-level ministry or management staff. When these people identify and pre-qualify mentoree candidates using the aforementioned characteristics and responsibilities, it is because they are familiar with and can vouch for them.
- Face-to-face marketing. This is successful in Sunday school classes or corporate divisions and is successful when the class instructors or division heads are sympathetic to the mentoring program.
- Printed announcements. Posted or circulated bulletins are a fair means of recruiting mentorees but only when local leaders have demonstrated approval and endorsement of the program. A brief written endorsement on the bulletin by an opinion leader is helpful.
- Satisfied customers. Mentors and mentorees have recommended the program to their friends and acquaintances. As in most marketing situations, satisfied customers encourage others by word of mouth.

Studies of age differences between mentor and mentorees show that, on average, mentors are fifteen years older than mentorees. Our youngest mentors are in their late twenties. However, we cannot always hold to the average difference as a criterion for matching because few mentoree candidates in their teen years have "formulated" or have a sense of life purpose which our kind of mentoring requires. This does not apply, however, when a teenager has a specific skill to be developed. Therefore, one of our mentors, Dan, was twenty-seven when Adam, a bright fifteen year old, expressed an interest in having an older person to whom he could be accountable and who also would be able to instruct him in Bible study methods. Dan was tailor-made for this assignment.

Studies of age differences between mentor and mentorees show that, on average, mentors are fifteen years older than mentorees.

Postmodernist thinking and behavior among below-thirty members of Generation X make them ideal for mentoring because they are predisposed to things spiritual. Their preoccupation with spiritualism, Wicca, mysticism, pantheism, and emotion-related motives for behavior, however, requires mentors to address these issues, sometimes before they can concentrate on purpose-oriented goals. Across the many churches where we have worked, about one fourth of younger mentorees hold to some form of postmodern lifestyle, which also influences how they interpret Scripture.

Our mentorees have spanned most age categories, the oldest being in their mid- to late-sixties. The younger ones in their twenties tend to focus primarily on what for them is a first-time sense of purpose in God. Those in middle age are usually reassessing the earlier years of their careers and now want to give attention to "more important matters." As we move up the age scale, we find pre-retirees and early retirees desiring to reestablish purposes they had earlier in life. These have yet to sing their best song, and we are happy to oblige them.

WHO MENTORS?

Mentorees do not exist for the purpose of giving mentors a job. In secular programs, mentors train less experienced employees for the benefit of the corporation; here, the reason for mentoring lies outside the personal interests of mentors and mentorees. Secular programs exist to perpetuate the corporate ethos, adapt to changing market conditions, meet customers' expectations, or increase shareholder value. In Christianity, the church's responsibility is to proclaim the kingdom and mature the saints, and the mentor is an instrument to make this happen. Each type of mentor, whether secular or religious, is servant to the mentoree who in response to mentoring has an obligation to grow to maturity.

Everitt and Murray-Hicks distinguish between the hallmarks of salaried master mentors and others who serve as volunteers.[2] The Christian authors cited above also use the Murray-Hicks criteria in their expanded lists of thirteen personal qualifications and nine interpersonal skills.

Thirteen personal qualifications of Christian mentors

- Has skills to focus on and meet mentoree needs
- Is willing to take a chance on the mentoree
- Can cultivate a relationship based on another's needs
- Has the respect of other Christians and those in the secular marketplace
- Has a network of resources and makes them available
- Is consulted by others and is a source of godly and worldly wisdom
- Talks and listens, being both teacher and counselor
- Has a consistent lifestyle
- Is able to diagnose and act on needs, seeing things in perspective
- Is biblically literate and skilled in biblical interpretation
- Expects and personally acts in terms of co-accountability
- Commits only to low-maintenance and high-impact mentorees
- Is process- and goal-oriented, being committed to results

Nine interpersonal skills of mentors

- Provides information, knowing things the mentoree does not
- Provides wisdom by applying truth and knowing what to do next
- Promotes skills based on mentoree needs

- Provides feedback with an informed view of mentoree's needs
- Coaches with skills relative to God's plan for mentoree's life
- Is a sounding board for asking questions and pre-testing ideas
- Is a trusted and respected friend without regard to schedule
- Helps devise broad-spectrum plans by giving perspective and advice
- Nurtures curiosity, opens doors, and shows possibilities

Recruiting Mentors: What Experience Has Taught

The mentor program coordinator prescreens trainee candidates according to the foregoing criteria. At the time of their interview, we summarize chapters 1 and 2 and provide opportunity for questions. Mentor-training candidates also write an autobiography, and we use this to match the most appropriate mentor with each mentoree.

Promising candidates come with endorsements by mid-level church leaders who have had working contact with them and vouch for their character and credibility.

Promising candidates come with endorsements by mid-level church leaders who have had working contact with them and vouch for their character and credibility. The larger the church, the less senior ministry staff can make informed recommendations from the pool of mentor candidates. This supports Murray's observations that those in top positions are often distant from and unfamiliar with many they otherwise think are good prospects.

Volunteer leaders are the second source of successful candidates. About one half from this source completed the mentor-training program. The third and often best source of recommendations is graduated mentors. There is no substitute for a satisfied customer! Seasoned mentors seem more qualified to judge the potential of trainees.

MATCHING MENTOR AND MENTOREE

A good match between mentor and mentoree requires more than surface impressions. Screening and recruiting has three parts: (1) matching on the frequency of qualifications listed above, (2) matching the autobiographies, and (3) prayer.

Matching Based on Qualifications

Figure 3 with its two tables is used in the matching of mentors and mentorees. The first table depicts a range of scores representing the number of characteristics and responsibilities that describe each the mentor and mentoree. The mentoree's score is located on the row where his or her score fits into one of the score-categories. The mentor's score is located on one of the columns, also having several score-categories. The two scores will meet in a single cell. For example, if the mentoree scores on only one successful characteristic, and the mentor qualifies on only one, then their respective scores would meet in the left uppermost cell of the table. If both of them had an individual score of eighteen, then their respective scores would meet in the right lowermost cell of the table.

The second table shows three areas having different degrees of shading. The area to the left and top of the table represents any combination of mentor and mentoree scores that are of lowest potential success; either the mentoree is unqualified or the mentor is unqualified. A successful mentor cannot produce good results in an unsuccessful mentoree. Similarly, a genius of a mentoree will not a good mentor make. The middle shaded area represents mentor-mentoree matches of moderate chance of success, and the lower right-hand corner of the table identifies those matches that have a high potential of success. We usually require additional information on either the mentor or mentoree if their match has a moderate chance of success.

Is this rocket science? Of course not, yet this simple management device enables us to make distinctions, using the information compiled on mentor and mentoree to match them to each other. The model has worked quite well, as long as it was backed up by autobiographies and prayer.

Matching Based on the Autobiography

Over the years of asking people to write autobiographies, we have discovered that once they start, memory recall produces amazing insights. The program coordinator uses the two autobiographies as an additional resource in matching mentor with mentoree.

Matching Mentoree
and Mentor by Levels of Maturity

Qualifications of Mentors

		1-3	4-6	7-9	10-12	13-15	16-18
Qualifications of Mentorees	**1-3**						3x18
	4-6						
	7-9						
	10-12						
	13-15						
	16-18						

In this chapter, numerous qualities of mentors and mentorees are used to evaluate their potential for performing their respective roles. The table above provides for a matching of mentor and mentoree in terms of how each "scores" by exhibiting up to eighteen qualities.

A cell exists for each combination of the mentor's and mentoree's scores. For example, if the mentoree exhibits three of the defining qualities, and the mentor exhibits eighteen, then the matched scores would fall in the uppermost right-hand cell of the table, as shown.

The table shown below has been divided into three sectors to connote a low, moderate, and high potential match between mentor and mentoree. The desire is to achieve matches between mentors and mentorees whose scores fall into the cluster of cells in the lower right-hand corner of the table.

Qualifications of Mentors

		1-3	4-6	7-9	10-12	13-15	16-18
Qualifications of Mentorees	**1-3**						
	4-6			Low Potential Match			
	7-9				Moderate Potential Match		
	10-12					High Potential Match	
	13-15						
	16-18						

Figure 3

Todd asked that I mentor him. I felt comfortable that I could work with him based on his autobiography and other qualifications. Nevertheless, I was hesitant to mentor him and instead assigned him to Len, one of the more seasoned mentors. After their second meeting Len reported back to me: "You wouldn't believe how similar his childhood and family was to what mine had been, even the same problems with my father and the same disruptive relationships. How did you know I was the perfect mentor for him?" I did not know the fit would be that good, but God answered my prayer for a good fit.

Carolyn confessed in her autobiography she was the most unlikely person to be a mentor, but I assigned Tina to her, anyway. "I don't like to counsel," Carolyn complained. "I don't like to presume I have answers or can guide a person's life, but I am a good listener." In her autobiography, Tina shared some of what she wanted out of the relationship: "I'm like a mother hen to so many of my peers, although I'm still in my twenties. They want to tell me their problems, perhaps because I'm a good listener. However, really, I'm hungry for someone to listen to me. Can you find me someone like that?"

Matching Based on the Mentor's Prayer

There was a time I struggled with how to pray for my own mentorees and what kind of a model prayer, if any, I could give to others I trained. The Mentor's Prayer was the result and has been read at the beginning of every training session. Mentors meditate on it as they go about their tasks. The first comment trainees have after reading it has usually been: "That's awesome; this is really an important ministry, isn't it?"

The Mentor's Prayer

Father, we beseech You by Your mercies that You reveal to us the sovereign purpose and divine destiny You have placed in each of these Your children in whose behalf we are delegated with this sacred mentoring trust. We sacrifice ourselves to partner with You, Sir, to see them as You see them. Hence, they will move from immaturity to maturity—genetically endowed with the perfect divine DNA and perfected according to Your plan. When matured, Father, they too will partner with You to perpetuate Your purposes for yet another generation. In this way, each of our and their divine moments will historically intersect the unfolding of the eternal course of Your kingdom.

Figure 4 portrays the three-way relationship between God, the mentor, and the mentoree.

ATYPICAL MENTOREES AND MENTORS————————————

The best laid plans of mice and men cannot anticipate what God in His sovereignty will do, simply because He is God and knows when He wants to exercise prerogatives that are exceptions to our rules. Those of us who plan want to be as precise and as comprehensive as

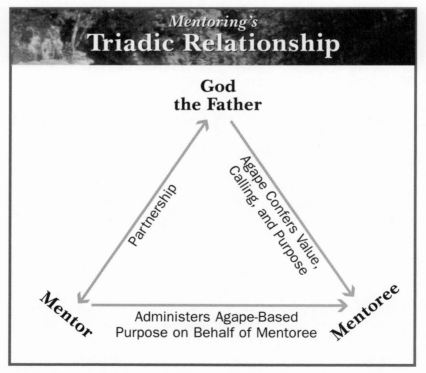

Figure 4

is practicable. However, we are sensitive to the principle that "man plans his ways, but the Lord directs his steps." This section shares some exceptions to well-laid plans.

Atypical Mentorees

Numerous characters in the Bible on first blush would not make the preferred list of high potential people for mentoring (according to our Western standards), nor qualify as low-maintenance and high-impact candidates. God in His wisdom sometimes chooses those of least qualification to serve His purposes and thereby confounds the wise of this world (1 Cor. 1:18–29).

Would we have chosen to mentor a fearful, stuttering, impulsive person such as Moses? (Certainly not if you were an Egyptian guard.) Would Joseph have made the cut, proud and flaunting as he was about his coat of many colors? Jacob's grabbing and scheming ways would disqualify him. What about the fearful Gideon who hid on the threshing floor and had a litany of excuses as to why he should not lead the three hundred? One look at Jeremiah's convulsions and wailing, and we become sick. I am still perplexed that Barnabas took Paul on, or that Paul continued to labor over the fearful, nauseous Timothy. Peter never seemed to tire: trying to put a stop to Jesus' ministry, the sophomoric plan to build three tabernacles on the Mount of Transfiguration, and, finally, the denials.

Are we missing something here, in that the faith of our fathers balanced precariously on the shoulders of men who would not have passed muster as modern mentoring candidates much less as mentors?

Presumption, based on the biblical record at least, suggests that residing inside some of the less wise, less noble, and less mighty members of our churches is a giant of the faith awaiting unveiling. Despite the use of logic to design biblical mentoring programs as we have here, the Father sometimes reserves for Himself the less reputable (1 Cor. 1:26–29) for whom the whole creation stands on tiptoes to see the revealed sons of God (Rom. 8:19). *Agape* is spontaneous and unmotivated, bestowing beauty where there is ugliness. God often circumvents humankind's efforts to excel, does away with the obvious, and confers value beyond wildest imaginations. Pray, therefore, before rejecting those who otherwise do not measure up to your standards of acceptance or the standards we recommend.

A period in my father's life illustrates both the atypical mentor and the atypical mentoree. Marshal Johns Oakes, several years before he married my mother, had the unseemly privilege of spending a year as guest of California's San Quentin State Penitentiary. Upon release, his parole officer, Maxey Bohr, befriended and mentored him back onto the straight and narrow. Maxey came to my family's home for dinner, met with us at family reunions, visited my father's service station at Ninth and Howard Streets in San Francisco, and otherwise became family.

During World War II, our family moved from the San Francisco area and Dad returned to his first love—ranching. In the beautiful Napa and Sonoma Valleys, he eventually acquired over eight thousand leased acres of land and raised hay, grain, and cattle. My father would go to the farm bureau to hire new farmhands, frequently choosing those who served jail time. I recall him working with these men, one after another, mentoring them, as Maxey Bohr previously had mentored him. They had a new father, a tough, demanding, often-irreligious boss, a mentor who wanted to know how they spent their weekends, and a friend who occasionally had to bail them out of the county jail after a drinking spree. He never gave up.

Our purpose was not to change them but merely to love them and discover the treasure we sensed was underneath the skin.

At my father's funeral, several hundred people gathered to pay their last respects. Scattered throughout the room were younger men, wives and children at their sides, who were ex-convicts—an unlikely group of mentorees who submitted to my father's rough mentoring ways.

A young family attended our church, and if ever there was a family cut from a different piece of cloth this one was it. The wife prepared and served nothing but natural foods; he was on a survivalist kick; and the kids were always full of beans. They were just different, and none of the church leaders, except my wife and me, pursued them as friends. Our purpose was not to change them but merely to love them and discover the treasure we sensed was underneath the skin. Our task was to mentor, discipline, correct, guide, counsel, and love. It went on for several years.

The husband eventually became an elder in our church, and his wife accepted an invitation to teach in the church's academy. Later, he was able to fit missionary trips into his vacations. He had always wanted to be a missionary. He would take his teenage son, Keith, on missionary trips, smuggling Bibles, medicines, and food into Cuba and then into Russia. At eighteen, the son, who had become active in Teen Mania, planned a solo trip around the world, moving from west to east using one of those one-direction airline tickets. His was a personal crusade to visit one missionary after another, minister, live with the people, and listen for God's voice to tell him the country to which he would return as a civil engineer and become a self-supporting missionary. Today, Keith is at Purdue University completing his engineering degree, soon to leave for Southeast Asia. They were, indeed, among the most unlikely mentorees my wife and I have had the privilege to serve, but *agape* proved its capacity to confer value across three generations.

Atypical Mentors

The story of Samuel is also the story of millions of elderly people in America whose churches have put them out to pasture. When Count Bismarck invented the first social security system in Germany, he set retirement at age sixty-five, knowing the average life expectancy at that time was sixty-seven. When President Roosevelt started America's social security program, age sixty-five stuck because it was convenient and few at that time gave thought to the long-term implications. The "infamous sixty-five" now tends to define people as inactive and useless—having lost youth, productivity, gainful employment, beauty, and strength.

When he was old and his sons failed to follow in his steps, the elders of Israel came to Samuel and told him they no longer wanted a judge in Israel, forcing him into retirement (1 Sam. 8). The American church has two views when it comes to the elderly. Like the society in which it exists, youth, beauty, strength, and productivity are the favored qualities in the church. And, like others in our culture, those who make it to sixty-five are shortly thereafter relegated to the pews, are enrolled in special age-graded programs that operate on a false set of assumptions, and are treated as if they were little puppies who ought not get in the way. The second assumption is that one's functional capacity has so decreased that it prevents further productivity in the church.

Return to Samuel. After receiving the word of the Lord, to let the elders in Israel have their king, Samuel, now forced into retirement, became a teacher. His school of the prophets, over many generations, outperformed in terms of impact all that Samuel had accomplished as a judge. You never know what a sovereign God can do with castoffs!

Stereotyping in the modern era is a cultural phenomenon and secondarily a religious one. We call it "pre-judging." The value of stereotyping is that it simplifies our characterization of complex situations, but that is also the greatest weakness of a stereotype—oversimplification. Stereotypes of the elderly assume that the callings and purposes of God cease to operate because of a person's age. The opposite of course is true.

The elderly, throughout the Old and New Testaments, receive respect because of their presumed wisdom and obedience to the law. The Hebrew elder stands side by side with the Homeric *gerontes* (gerontology), the Spartan *presbys* (presbytery), the Roman *senatus* (senator), and the Arab *sheikh*—all honorific, held in high regard, and serving as a source of authority in social, family and spiritual matters.[3]

Psalms 92:10–15, in reference to older adults, declares that God holds in high esteem one's horn (of power). He freshly anoints the elder with oil, gives new blooms to those who are righteous, and allows them to thrive in the house of the Lord. In old age they still produce fruit, are full of sap and freshness, and attest that the Lord is upright.[4] Psalms 103:104–5 reaffirms that "He redeems your life from the Pit, surrounds you with steadfast love and mercy. He satisfies you with good things in the prime of life, so that your youth is renewed like the eagle's." The passage implies that like the new crop of feathers eagles put on following a molt, it is not possible to judge their age.[5]

> *Stereotypes of the elderly assume that the callings and purposes of God cease to operate because of a person's age. The opposite of course is true.*

Moses led his people until he was 120 years of age. John was likely 100 when he wrote his first letter. Caleb was about 80 when he began to inherit his particular piece of land in Canaan. There are many other examples, all sufficing to show that in a community of believers, many elderly are productive, revered, and useful to the spiritual welfare of the community and many others can be recruited to renewed vitality.

George Barna in 1990 wrote that churches have to stop thinking of the elderly as requiring ministry but rather as a group of potential lay ministers. Seniors are not a population seeking to sit back and watch life pass them by, but rather a group desirous of actively participating in ministry.[6]

Barna in 1990 wrote that churches have to stop thinking of the elderly as requiring ministry but rather as a group of potential lay ministers.

Joanne returned to the States following her husband's death after they had spent more than twenty years as missionaries in Korea. One of the pastors recommended that she enroll for mentor training, and it did not take long before she knew she had found new purpose in life—to mentor others. She joined with another missions-oriented mentor, who was also in his sixties, and they began to mentor a couple nearing retirement. Within several months, Roy and Rhonda committed their lives to the mission field, enrolled in the mentor-training program and a foreign missions perspective course, and made plans to attend the Cross Roads Program of Youth With A Mission.

A psychiatrist friend is medical director for a program of suicidal and violent youth, and he related the story of a program in a southeastern state that allowed a "granny" to visit the unit. No sooner would she enter the room than disturbed youths would run to get her a chair, gather around her, caress her gray hair, politely chat with her, and listen as she told stories of her family. As long as the granny was on the unit, there was peace and quiet. When she left, the noise and aggressiveness returned to prior levels. I asked my friend how many grannies he could use in his local program. He said that if they would do the basic mentor training, he could put a dozen to work immediately.

These are the unlikely mentors, in thousands of churches, awaiting training. For years, they have served and learned the art of *agape*. As they mentor, their youth returns like that of the eagle and their horns fill to overflowing.

My last story is of a man who retired from two careers before beginning his last one as a mentor of giants in the halls of power. Following World War II, Abraham Vereide journeyed to

Washington, D.C., after careers as a Methodist circuit-riding pastor in the mountain states and an executive stint with Goodwill Industries. He memorized the names and photos of members of Congress and stood on the steps of the capitol. As congressmen and senators came up the wide steps, Vereide stepped forward, called them by name, and introduced himself. "Sir, do mind if I ask you a few questions?" If they were willing, he continued. "Do you believe in God?" "Do you believe the Bible is the Word of God?" "Do you know what the Bible says about your responsibilities as an elected leader of the people?" "May I have fifteen minutes once a week to share with you what those responsibilities are?"

When the answer to the final question was "yes," Vereide was in every office, once a week, mentoring men and women at the highest levels of government. Out of that simple beginning came the Senate, House, and White House prayer breakfasts and, on an international scale, the International Christian Leadership and the National Prayer Breakfasts. Vereide birthed a veritable web of non-sectarian Christian influences worldwide that continues unabated throughout the highest levels of influence to this day, proving that when mentoring is "in season," the impact can be enormous, even among atypical mentors.

CHAPTER TEN

The Sponsoring Organization

FEW MODERN BOOKS ON ORGANIZATIONAL MANAGEMENT FAIL TO HAVE A SECTION ON VISION AND ITS VALUE FOR THE ORGANIZATION. VISION IS WHAT LEADERS HOLD OUT AS THE IDEALIZED FUTURE toward which the organization moves. In accordance with the vision, organizations formulate one or more missions, or strategies, for moving the organization forward. Vision points toward the future; mission moves it there. Once we articulate what we consider the correct vision for the church, we will know whether biblical mentoring enjoys a reasonable fit.

George Barna sees vision as the critical element for *Marketing the Church*.[1] Guy Kawasaki promotes visionary "evangelism" as the key to *Selling the Dream* of a world filled with Apple Computers.[2] Burt Nanus defines visionary leadership as the performance of a person who has a realistic, credible, and attractive future for the organization.[3] Tom Peters quotes Father Theodore Hesburgh, former president of Notre Dame University, as saying that "The very essence of leadership is [that] you have to have a vision. [It has] to be a vision you articulate clearly and forcefully on every occasion. . . ."[4] James Collins and Jerry I. Porris credit vision as the moving force of organizations *Built to Last*.[5] Collins has spoken to leaders of mega-churches with the result that visionary senior pastors go away energized to implement Collins's BHAG—the "big hairy audacious goal" that visualizes a worthy future.

Noble people have noble visions. Dawson Trotman, founder of the Navigators, envisioned during World War II every military base

and naval ship having on it a Bible study and prayer group led by
Navigator-trained servicemen and women. Loren Cunningham
started Youth With A Mission and envisioned waves of short-term
missionaries spilling over the shores of every tribe and tongue, and
hundreds of thousands now do. Pat Robertson's *700 Club* and
Christian Broadcasting Network have expanded to the four corners
of the globe and added an L-1011 flying hospital, Operation
Blessing, and world-class Regent University. The Billy Graham
Evangelistic Association for over five decades has taken crusades to
dozens of nations and to audiences of billions through satellite up-
links. Bill Bright energized Campus Crusade for Christ on college
and university campuses starting during the 1950s, and later
promoted the showing of the *Jesus* film to millions in
practically every nation on the globe. German-born
evangelist Reinhard Bonnke preaches to one half
million people at a time in Africa, has a public
address system capable of broadcasting to a million,
and envisions the day when he will see one million
people simultaneously make decisions for Christ in
a public meeting. These and hundreds of others
capture the commitment of thousands of others who
invest in their visions.

The phenomenon of vision is not dependent on the truth of the vision. . . . The formulation and implementation of vision are available to all.

The phenomenon of vision is not dependent on
the truth of the vision. Those mentioned above
had noble purposes. Others have not. Sigmund
Freud had a vision of a psychoanalyzed world; Josef Stalin of a
socialist world; Adolph Hitler of a dictatorially controlled world;
and the Meddalin Cartel of a narcotized world. Any venture can
be successful predicated on how well the vision is articulated and
gathers others who share and work for it. Hence, the Bible with
its gospel of the kingdom is pitted against Hitler's *Mein Kampf*,
Marx's *Das Kapital*, Darwin's *Origin of the Species*, and Machiavelli's
The Prince—one vision against another. The formulation and
implementation of vision are available to all.

Vision is value neutral. There is nothing noble about vision
itself. Further, even in the case where one has a noble vision, the
means of implementing it, returning to the emphasis of chapter
1, can vary in terms of *eros, nomos,* or *agape*. Let this sink in. Every
Christian leader who wants to do big things for God is capable of
doing them from any of these three motifs or some mixture

among them. Church history leaves little doubt on this score, and I address the manner these three motifs influence organizations.

<hr>

BIBLICAL VISION

What kind of vision of the institutional church is worthy of biblical mentoring such as I have described? Is there a preeminent vision that emerges from biblical truth? Is there a pivotal issue on which Christendom can agree and stand, or is any vision acceptable? A core vision is necessary, for, without it, everything else the church does is unrestrained, according to Proverbs 29:18, subject to the whims of man, and derives from the surrounding society.

The Ultimate Vision of the Church

Vision outlives leaders; its realization lies beyond the talent and energy of any one person, and this certainly is true of the ultimate vision of the church. The perfected vision, already a completed fact in prophetic time, is expressed in Isaiah 6:1–3, Numbers 14:21, and Isaiah 66:18–23 and states that God's glory fills the earth. He has spoken it! The creation declares His glory. His glory is everywhere!

The perfecting dimension of the vision is something still in progress, as in Habakkuk 2:14: "The whole earth will be filled with the knowledge of the glory of the Lord, as the waters cover the sea." The greatest passion of God's heart is to be glorified! John Piper, senior pastor of Minneapolis's Bethlehem Baptist Church, has summarized this concisely.

> He created us for His glory (Isaiah 43:7); He called Israel to be His people for His glory (Isaiah 49:3); Jesus lived (John 17:4) and died (John 12:27–28; Romans 3:25–26) and rose (Romans 6:4) and reigns (Philippians 2:11) for the glory of God; He chose us before the foundation of the world for His glory (Ephesians 1:4–6); He forgives us for His glory (Psalms 25:11; Isaiah 43:25); He works through us for His glory (1 Peter 4:11); He calls us to do all things for His glory (1 Corinthians 10:31); His aim is that the earth will be covered with the knowledge of

His glory the way the waters cover the sea (Habakkuk 2:14);
and in the age to come that the glory of the Lord alone will be
the awesome light of endless days (Revelation 21:23).[6]

Pastor Piper surprised his audience by adding that the
conversion of people by missionaries was not preeminent; born
again is not the end goal; rather, people coming to the faith are a
means of giving glory to God. This distinction, pitting means
against ends, reinforces the difference between vision and
mission. Vision is the supreme end. Mission is the means of
getting there. The mission of an organization, in one or more
pieces, is the manageable bite-sized way the organization goes
about the business of reaching the vision.[7]

Ultimate Vision and Mentoring as Mission

A complete gospel of the kingdom requires, as developed in
chapter 2, both internal and external emphases. The external
emphasis takes the gospel to the hinterlands and makes disciples
of all nations. This brings glory to God and makes His glory
known throughout all the earth. The internal emphasis commits
to maturing Christians and prepares them to participate in some
form of the external emphasis. This too brings glory to God and
makes His glory known throughout all the earth.

Paul left little doubt in 1 Corinthians 3:8–17 that leaders must
take seriously the building of each believer's life on the foundation
of Christ, with the goal that each believer be a suitable temple of
the Holy Spirit. To ignore this mandate, Paul wrote, incurred God's
personal destruction of the careless leader. Christians who are high
maintenance and low impact hardly are equipped to make the
glory of God known and are hardly able to give glory to God themselves. Terms more graphic express that church pews filled with
acorns full of permanent potential are hardly to God's glory.

The biblical mentoring program begins with an internal focus
on member maturity, but it has the long view, or external focus,
in mind by launching matured members who live out their
purposes in God. The manner in which the church is organized,
however, influences the effectiveness of a mentoring program.
Not all structures contribute equally to smooth mentoring
program development.

Many leaders in the 1980s felt the era of "super religious leaders" was closing. The downfall of several national ministries likely contributed to this conclusion. Shrinking memberships in mainline denominations also suggested the organizational landscape was changing. Several trends help explain some of the changes.

Parishioner Spirituality, Personal Autonomy, and Pastoral Insecurities

The futurists we cited in the introduction agree on trends relevant to religious life of the twenty-first century: spirituality will increase, and individuals will assume more control of their own religious education. This is either boon or threat to the institutional church. It is a boon when serious-minded people seek involvement in church programs, and it is a threat if they seek competing alternatives outside the church.

Vineyard Fellowship founder John Wimber, in the later years of his ministry, was consultant to hundreds of churches and thousands of pastors on church growth and organizational management. He shared at a national leadership conference what he saw as a critical problem in the contemporary church in the light of certain demographic trends.

Wimber observed that one of the major threats to church growth was in the pulpit itself, where many pastors feared what they perceived as highly competent members vying for leadership in the church. It can be intimidating to preach to members who may be more biblically literate, are not afraid to challenge inaccuracies in biblical interpretation, and in many instances know as much if not more about corporate management than many pastors know. *Leadership Journal* testifies to the same observation—that seminarians taught to minister are deficient in training others to lead.[8]

The Southern Baptist Convention's LeaderLife Program specifically recruits senior pastors to mentor junior pastors in the area of leadership development from within the congregations. Mentoring is a strategy for assuring the stability of the individual congregation in terms of having mature leaders and ensuring its continuity over time.

While instructive, Wimber's observations are affected by other forces that operate in today's religious environment.

Competition and lessening loyalties

Religious organizations outside the institutional church, referred to as *parachurch*, often compete quite successfully with the institutional church for member loyalty. They introduce new ideas into the church and challenge traditional ways of thinking and doing things. These organizations frequently are founded and led by Christians not formally trained in seminaries. Contemporary seekers often find them attractive because their leaders are people of the "real world" rather than people of the cloth. Ex-football coach Bill McCartney of Promise Keepers is a key example. Hundreds of such organizations have challenged the loyalties of otherwise faithful church members. A key feature of these organizations is that they employ highly effective strategies from the secular sector to meet religious goals and frequently do so without compromising Christian principles or practices. Promise Keepers, for example, recognizes that the long-term success of its efforts is not in successive rallies but church-based accountability groups and the mentoring of developing Christians by more mature ones.

Parishioners are not committed to denominations and denominational doctrine as they once were, and the opportunities for shopping from church to church have increased. Fewer people are born into a denomination and therefore do not inherit the doctrine of their parents or grandparents. Denominational churches see this trend and deliberately remove denominational identity from their church signs and literature. The child born today is more likely to acquire a personal faith from a marketplace of options, going as an adult from place to place to meet personal and family needs.

Hundreds of parachurch organizations have challenged the loyalties of otherwise faithful church members.

The decreasing loyalty to a denomination "frees" an individual to seek other means of expression, not the least of which is to look deeply within for a more "authentic" expression of relationship with God. Hence, mentoring in terms of a more personalized divine purpose may take the place of a confirmation ceremony following a period of indoctrination to a denominational catechism.

Secular changes and emerging church structures

The aforementioned flatter corporate structures that began to work their way into the institutional church in the 1980s provided more opportunities for individual creativity, again "freeing people" to exercise their spiritual gifts. Jesus, it will be recalled, considered customs and traditions good if they reminded us of our heritage (the care of parents, for instance), but they could also stifle personal creativity. Sociological and management trends, while external to the church, still condition church members to anticipate similar opportunities for self-expression and living out their faith.

Stanford University professor of management Jim Collins distinguishes between the more traditional visionary leader that is charismatic and goal-oriented and the contemporary visionary organization that surges ahead with many people in tow who themselves are movers and shakers.[9]

Visionary companies can have one CEO after another, Collins notes, and all may be strong leaders, but the company has a vision independent of the CEO. Vision has a life of its own. Such an organization draws all employees into a highly coordinated effort to work for something that is beyond them and will live in perpetuity.

A variation on the visionary organization is the visionary division—a subpart of an organization that outperforms all other divisions and may even be lost or go unnoticed in an otherwise lackluster corporation. As long as flatter church structures provide for individual creativity, then creative volunteers are free to develop highly effective mentoring programs that can have a redemptive and restorative impact on an otherwise ineffectual church.

STRUCTURE AS *NOMOS*, *EROS*, AND *AGAPE*

We described three kinds of mentoring programs in chapter 1, and churches similarly can have an overriding ethos of *nomos*, *eros*, and *agape*.

Nomos-Governed Structures

Organizations can be extremely legalistic, given to strict adherence to rules, inflexible as to procedures, intolerant of

creativity, and controlling by fear of punishment. The structure
and function is authoritarian. These are *nomos*.

Nomos also can govern churches through its leaders. The
post–World War II studies of the so-called authoritarian person-
ality showed that no profession was exempt from having its
authoritarian leaders. The mentoring program in such a church
is more by indoctrination, with the purpose of training new
recruits to assume predetermined positions. There would be
little attention given to the fulfillment of God's calling and
purpose in a person's life. In fact, leaders would be the sole deter-
miners of God's calling and purposes for the individual. I recall a
good friend, the pastor of a fifteen hundred-member church who
explained that seminary professors and district superintendents
recommended that as soon as he took office, he was to "grab
control and not let go."

The fate of mentoring programs in *nomos*-type churches is of
several possibilities. They will not organize in the first place,
since delegating authority to mentors makes them similar in
function (thus potential competitors) to pastors or elders. Once
organized, however, they would receive little publicity or die
through benign neglect. The third possibility is that they will
become a pawn of senior staff, to promote rigid church policy.

Eros-Governed Structures

The church structured around *eros* is self-serving and uses
members to achieve corporate goals. The atmosphere among
members also is one of self-aggrandizement and self-gratification.
Division directors will posture themselves to get a larger budget
at the expense of other divisions; individuals will try to become
the soloist in the choir, capitalize on the pastor's time, or become
the family that controls church policy.

The mentoring program in an *eros*-ruled church will not function to optimize the callings and purposes of God. Rather, leaders
emotionally vandalize mentorees by assigning them responsibilities that have nothing to do with their unique calling and
purposes in God. These members want to serve God, and they
willingly volunteer for one task after another. The result is that
someone else's program benefits but not necessarily that which
God wants in the mentoree's life.

A college-aged man attended a meeting of church leaders. I happened to mention that the institutional church often is like a gigantic astronomical black hole, one of those immense gravitational forces that sucks up every bit of cosmic dust in its path and then spits it out some jillion miles away on the other side of the universe. Several weeks after that meeting the college student called my office and asked if we could have lunch. There, away from parents and church leaders, he confessed he was some of the cosmic dust, assigned one responsibility after another, for no reason other than he wanted to serve God. The problem, however, was that he was doing poorly in school, and God had made it clear he was to devote his life as a family counselor in behalf of neglected children. He wanted to be a mentoree and regain balance and excellence of performance in his classes. One of the first tasks I assigned was to list all volunteer activities and rank them in priority order. He was to choose the top two activities and dump the remainder. In twelve months, he made the dean's list.

In organizations ruled by *nomos* or *eros*, willing members are recruited, overworked, and given an indefinite sabbatical when they are emotionally and physically spent.

Agape-Governed Structures

The church characterized by *agape* is a joy to behold. "They knew they were Christians by the *agape* they had for each other." The *agape* church is a "one another church": love one another, encourage one another, support one another, comfort one another, seek not one's own interests but that of another. It is dedicated to every other person's success in the kingdom.

Agape is humble and is aware that every member is the recipient of conferred value by an unmotivated spontaneous God. The leaders know that God has designated for the church a set of missions predicated on giving God glory. They know that as part of those missions each member has a unique place and role to play in the kingdom. The mentoring program brings this about.

Agape *programs in non-*agape *structures*
The reference above to Collins's recognition of visionary divisions or departments in a company applies to biblical mentoring

programs in churches whose primary motif may be *eros* or *nomos*. These divisions will excel beyond the performance of all others. They often set a standard for others, and happily, all can eventually benefit. Visionary divisions are more the exception than the rule, and when they do exist, they become the targets of those given to gossip, rumor, slander, and defamation.

A visionary mentoring program operating in an otherwise non-visionary church, or one ruled by *eros* or *nomos,* will incur the wrath of envious staff members or volunteer leaders, especially when the program is successful. Such a program can be salt, light, and yeast to an otherwise non-kingdom church. A senior mentor once bemoaned the practices of some of the leaders in his church, citing biblical principles to support his criticism. I asked what he intended to do, and he replied: "I'm going to be an insurgent kingdom man, working undercover right here to bring one person at a time into the presence and will of God." A division manager in a larger urban church reported: "The mentoring program is producing quality people that will infect in the best way possible the mediocrity that exists elsewhere in the church."

Program-Based and Open Structures

Most churches today are "program-based" and serve as many seekers as they can. The pattern in this structure involves 15 percent of the members who do all the work. Mentors come from this 15 percent and in turn mentor others who likewise will become part of the 15 percent in the future.

The cell church is a mentoring church, with each cell leader taking a personal responsibility for the fulfillment of the potential of those in his or her cell.

The larger the church, the more difficult it is to convert the organization into what James Rutz calls the *Open Church*,[10] and what writers such as Ralph Neighbor[11] and William A. Beckham[12] call the cell-based church. The difference between the centralized authority of the program-based church and the decentralized authority of the cell-based church is in its orientation to the concept and practice of mentoring. The cell church is a mentoring church, with each cell leader taking a personal responsibility for the fulfillment of the potential of those in his or her cell.

True as it may be that the kingdom of God is not a democracy (a point some authoritarian pastors are fond of making), the New Testament, in the view of many church historians, remains rather silent concerning the organizational structure of the institutional church. Beckham's *The Second Reformation* differs from this view and instead articulates a systematic theology of church structure. Jesus did lay, according to Beckham, a foundation for the structure of the primitive first-century church that gives a prominent place to mentoring. Christians journeyed from home to home, were forced into the catacombs, fled into all of Asia, and spread the gospel to the then-known civilized world in the first one hundred years. The decentralized structure required an active fivefold ministry as described in Ephesians 4. Believers submitted to the eldership, grew to maturity, and met the needs of other Christians.[13]

The growth in the number of churches with greater delegation of authority will more readily accommodate mentoring efforts. Here, maturity flourishes without threatening leaders since leaders see church growth as a function of a multiplicity of leaders at different levels.

WHERE IN THE ORGANIZATION DOES MENTORING FIT?

Churches and other organizations will vary in terms of where senior staff members place the mentoring program in the organizational structure.

Discipling and Mentoring

Those who accept that mentoring is a cut above the usual form of discipling classes are also likely to assume it would follow discipling and become Discipling II. In churches where discipling provides for a continuing relationship between a more experienced person and one less experienced, mentoring is the next logical step.

The Education Program and Mentoring

The education program in most churches is didactic and patterned after secular models of instruction. Mentoring, as I have described it, would not find a home in this area. Paul's instruction to Timothy signals a break with the didactic:

> Look Timothy, you've been teaching this new group of converts almost like you were taught in synagogue school, sitting, listening, and asking questions. It is time you now choose from among your students those who have already proved themselves faithful. Pull them aside and impart yourself to them. Invest a deposit of yourself into their lives in an ongoing inter-active manner, taking advantage of the words of prophecy that were spoken over them and on which you will build them up into their purposes in God's plans for their lives. (2 Tim. 2:2, paraphrased)

Pastoral Ministry and Leadership Development

There is great advantage to defining the mentoring program as a hybrid of both the pastoral ministries and leadership development efforts. First, mentorees are encouraged to exercise their God-given purposes, and this renders them ministers in a manner that they will build up the church wherever they are. It may be in the local church; it may be in their places of business, family, or play. Second, mentoring produces a person who leads at some point within the body of Christ, for I am of the belief that properly mentored people are leaders relative to their gifts and talents. True, they join with others in the sense of being interdependent, but in the performance of their purposes, they are elevated to leadership.

For this reason, senior pastors should have a personal and corporate interest in the success of the mentoring program, for it is from trained mentors that they will have a corps of trusted and capable people who can stand alongside them and others in formal leadership to contribute to the stability and continuity of the organization. Leadership development is a critical need in today's churches, and I know of no other way to achieve this kind of goal than through person-to-person mentoring.

I have concluded from my experience that while senior pastors may mentor those immediately under them (associate and assistant pastors), they should personally delegate the responsibility to coordinate the mentoring program to someone from the congregation who has had management experience. The program coordinator reports directly to the senior pastor or one of the associate or assistant pastors. It is unwise for the coordinator to be under the authority of one whose philosophy is inconsistent with the model I have offered.

Properly mentored people are leaders relative to their gifts and talents.

Biblical Mentoring Outside of the Church

Biblical mentoring is by no means restricted to the institutional church. The principles I have described are applicable to many kinds of organizations. I have shown that the criteria for choosing mentors and mentorees in secular organizations are remarkably similar to those used in churches. It is not a large step, therefore, to apply them across other types of organizations, both Christian and secular.

Some have asked whether the same principles have a place in businesses. There are two answers. First, after forty years of working the secular environment, I have found that when the mentoring person meets another Christian who is seeking growth in purpose, the occasion for a mentoring relationship exists, even in a secular organization. There is nothing so exciting for mentors than to help brothers or sisters grow in their place of work, knowing that lights will shine brighter. Second, there is growing evidence that a new paradigm in worker relations is welcome. For too long the business environment has suffered from unethical, calloused, and selfish behavior among employees. *Eros* has corrupted every sector of the marketplace, and many leaders realize the limits of its usefulness. The reader who is involved mostly in the business environment knows the usefulness of the *agape* model for worker and employee relations, productivity, worker loyalty, and employee assistance programs. Hence, *agape*-oriented mentors should find a home in many secular organizations.

CHAPTER ELEVEN

Implementing the Mentoring Program

THIS CHAPTER PROVIDES A MODEL FOR IMPLEMENTING A MENTORING PROGRAM USING THE MATERIAL OF PRIOR CHAPTERS. MODELS ARE ABBREVIATIONS OF REALITY. LIKE SKELETONS, THEY HELP US organize the details that are unique to each local situation.

PREPROGRAM DEVELOPMENT

Organizations go through several stages of development in the process of becoming stable, productive, and enduring. Some organizations are start-ups, where survival is the major issue. Others have advanced to a stage of testing their products and services, and the more seasoned ones are stable and capable of exploring new ventures. While this summary is far from exhaustive, if you understand the basic dynamics of each phase, you will have a sense of when it is "safe" to begin a mentoring program and when it is more risky.

The Basal Phase of Development

In start-up organizations, which also include new churches, a period of one to two years is devoted to survival. The issues of greatest concern include cash flow, start-up capital, first-year operating expenses, leadership structure, human resource recruitment and development, facilities and maintenance, determination of market(s) and marketing, and, of course, the definition of the organization's mission. All of these are untested and considered negotiable. In this phase, the focus is on exploring the essentials, and wise leaders know this is not the time to be aggressive and overcommit members to more than organizational survival tasks.

To quote the King of Siam when he addressed Anna in the popular musical, *The King and I*, this is a time of "getting to know you." During this basal phase, a limited amount of consideration has been given to a mentoring program mission statement, the coordinator has been chosen, the requirements and qualifications for mentor trainees and mentorees have been formulated, and a recruitment strategy is put into practice.

The greatest use of the mentoring program during this phase is to support the organization's start-up activities. Leaders particularly may mentor others who play an important role in early survival, such as division managers. The purpose here is to give stability and prepare for corporate continuity during the first two years of the organization.

The Consolidation Phase

The consolidation phase is for testing the efficiency and effectiveness of an organization's subsystems to determine their ability to function and carry out the stated missions of the organization. These include assessing the adequacy of facilities, management, staffing, markets, and cash flow. If the mentoring program began in the basal phase, then it too is undergoing testing along with other church programs.

I do not recommend starting a mentoring program during the consolidation period. This is not the time to commit the organization to new challenges, but, as the name implies, to consolidate earlier efforts.

The end of the consolidation period comes when leaders, basing their judgments on measurement criteria, jointly agree they can move into the future with confidence.

The Organizational Phase

The organizational phase is one of maturity and allows for expanding the original services, broadening the market, and experimenting with new services or products, including mentor program development. Survival no longer is an issue, and corporate stability and continuity are givens. If mentoring began in the basal stage to assure corporate survival, now is the time to expand it to include recruitment and training of new generations of mentors and mentorees.

PROGRAM DEVELOPMENT

Figure 5 summarizes the steps we follow in getting the program started and operating. Each program has its unique features, but the sequence of tasks indicated here represents a fair average of our experience.

Clarifying and Advertising the Mission

In one church where I planned a major mentor training effort, I made a presentation first to the board of directors for their formal approval, and then to the pastoral staff to answer questions pertaining to program goals and whether they would duplicate or conflict with existing activities.

The program mission statement should be in writing, enjoy consensus from the organization's leaders, be available for conceptual and emotional ownership by those who will carry it out, and be visible for everyone who enters the church or business. The program's mission statement must be consistent with the overall mission and goals of the parent organization.

The mission statement only covers the basic activity of the program. It never is an operations plan.

The mission statement
The mentoring program assists eligible candidates to achieve skills to become mentors and assists them to mentor others to reach their God-ordained calling and purposes.

There is great value for all church members and visitors to see mission statements stated clearly and displayed throughout the church building, or at least published in a booklet that is available to all who wish to know more about the program. Staff

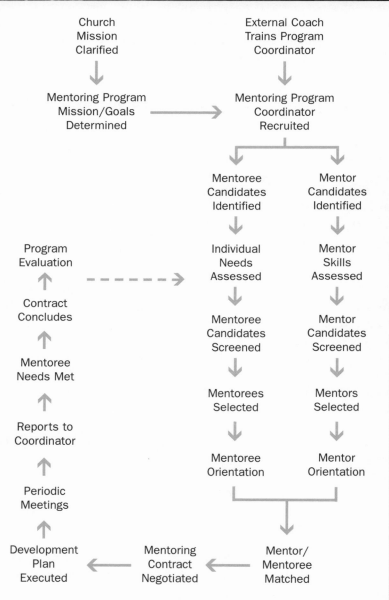

Mentoring
Development Process

Church
Mission
Clarified

↓

External Coach
Trains Program
Coordinator

↓

Mentoring Program
Mission/Goals
Determined

→

Mentoring Program
Coordinator
Recruited

Mentoree
Candidates
Identified

Mentor
Candidates
Identified

↓

↓

Program
Evaluation

↑

Individual
Needs
Assessed

Mentor
Skills
Assessed

↓

↓

Contract
Concludes

↑

Mentoree
Candidates
Screened

Mentor
Candidates
Screened

↓

↓

Mentoree
Needs Met

↑

Mentorees
Selected

Mentors
Selected

↓

↓

Reports to
Coordinator

↑

Mentoree
Orientation

Mentor
Orientation

Periodic
Meetings

↑

↓

Development
Plan
Executed

←

Mentoring
Contract
Negotiated

←

Mentor/
Mentoree
Matched

Figure 5

members often are required to memorize and recite the organization's mission statements.

Jesus' instructions to the disciples had a consistency about them. We imagine his "mission statement" burned in their minds whenever they went on missionary journeys: First, pray the Father's blessing on the village. Second, determine what the health, hunger, and emotional needs of the village are and meet those needs. Third, proclaim the kingdom.

The mission statement only covers the basic activity of the program. It never is an operations plan.

Essential Program Staff

The program coordinator is the manager of the mentoring program. If the program develops with help from outside the church, then an external coach is important to provide ongoing assistance to the local coordinator.

Program coordinator

The program coordinator is a leader with management or operations skills and is accountable to the senior pastor or pastor's designee. The coordinator is responsible for assuring the program's compliance with the church's vision and mission and its coordination with other church departments and activities. Based on Barna's earlier research findings concerning the lack of management experience among pastors, my vote for choice of a program coordinator is one who has had tested and proven management experience in the secular marketplace. Ideally, the candidate will have worked in management, may have had team-building or human relations experience, and appreciates the need for co-accountability on the part of both mentor and mentoree for assigned tasks.

External coach

The external coach's contribution is especially important for new programs, assisting the organization to screen candidates for the coordinator job and make recommendations of the most likely candidate. The external coach is not a mentor in the local church but rather a technical resource, local or distant, who is responsive to program trouble-shooting and serves more as a consultant than a participant. (The qualifications of the coach appear in the appendix.) Much of the coach's help will be by phone, fax, or e-mail. Face-to-face meetings occur on an as-needed basis.

Mentor and Mentoree Recruitment

Mentor and mentoree candidates come into the program along parallel paths. The program coordinator may wish to work with mentors first—identifying and training them. After training the first tier of mentors, the coordinator recruits, screens, and matches mentorees with mentors.

Recruiting and training mentors

Senior or mid-level staff or existing mentors are the ones most likely to identify future mentors. Selection criteria are in chapter 9 and consist of qualifications and responsibilities, the completion of an autobiography, and the candidate's agreement with chapters 1 and 2 and the Mentor's Prayer.

We have used two training formats. The first is a classroom setting over a six-month period, meeting twice a month for sessions of two to three hours. The other involves intensive seminars of fourteen hours held over three successive days—three hours each on Thursday and Friday evenings and eight hours on Saturday. We reserve Saturday afternoon for a practicum involving role-playing, problem solving, and group responses to various hypothetical scenarios of mentoring situations. The program coordinator provides counsel on an on-demand basis for each graduated mentor.

Those trained as mentors return to a variety of pursuits either in their church work or in their places of employment. Often, they receive training with the express purpose of increasing the effectiveness of responsibilities other than mentoring others. After the training, however, at least one half of the graduates consider mentoring a calling and purpose and want to mentor on a regular basis. Most pastors would welcome knowing that promotion of a mentoring program had this kind of promise in providing the church with a group of capable workers.

Recruiting and training mentorees

Identifying mentoree candidates, assessing their needs and goals, and screening them leads to final selection. Just as some mentors do not make the cut, there are also mentoree candidates who must, like John Mark, because of his failed relationship with Paul, wait for another time.

The program coordinator contributes to the final selection by meeting with the newly matched mentor and mentoree at their first meeting. In a way, the mentor and coordinator are making a final evaluation of the mentoree. The mentoree is asked to explain why he or she wants to be mentored and to describe desired needs and goals. The mentoree provides evidence of his or her commitment to the mentoring relationship and expresses an understanding of accountability to the mentor.

In the initial interview, the opportunity exists to get new information that was not evident from earlier queries, perhaps of a hidden character flaw that would require early intervention. The story of Randy's meeting with the mentor and program coordinator is a good example.

The mentoree provides evidence of his or her commitment to the mentoring relationship and expresses an understanding of accountability to the mentor.

Randy was thirty-four, the manager of a statewide volunteer youth program, and had most of the credentials one looks for in a promising mentoree. He had a good Christian wife and was college-educated, a professional manager, articulate, literate, and, most of all, he really wanted to be mentored so that one day he could mentor others. The senior mentor matched with Randy was a college mathematics professor, a retired career army full colonel, and a member of his church's board of directors. The match seemed perfect; however, both the mentor and coordinator sensed a problem that was uncovered about an hour into the meeting.

Randy had a cavalier attitude about extramarital sexual transgressions he confessed to us. He knew he had harmed his wife, but, in his words, "She seems to be getting over it, but it's taking longer than I would like, because her lack of trust in me interferes with our sexual relations." As they probed, it was obvious that Randy was insensitive to the idea of a personal holiness and to the biblical standards concerning this. The mentor and coordinator were disturbed. They told Randy how they felt and about the possibility that Randy might not be ready for mentoring. He stopped just short of begging for admission to the program.

The mentor's assignment to Randy was to read R. C. Sproul's *The Holiness of God* and to report to the mentor what he had learned. Unless the book impacted his life, mentoring would not take place, and Randy would be sent back to an accountability group until he got his act together.

Executing the Development Plan

The development plan begins by matching the mentoree's needs and goals to the mentor's experience, skills, and talents. The mentoree's needs and goals are the content of all the tasks he or she will be required to complete.

The mentor's assignments vary. There may be materials to read, seminars or conferences to attend, interviews with outside parties, written reports to complete, meetings where the mentoree and his or her spouse have dinner with the mentor and his or her spouse, a trip the two take together, or teaming on a joint project. One mentoree wanted assistance on how to conduct a job search. His assignment was to go on an information-gathering campaign and inquire of selected CEOs of opportunities in the town where he lived. He studied interview techniques. The mentor called six CEOs and asked if they would be willing to spend twenty no-pressure-to-hire minutes with the mentoree. They agreed, and the mentoree made the appointments. After the interviews were completed, the mentoree reported to the mentor for debriefing and the next set of instructions.

Another mentoree was having a hard time determining God's guidance and wanted mentoring for this. The mentor began with a simple question: "How much vacation time do you have coming at your place of work?"

"Seven days," she replied.

"Good; the first thing we are going to do is be sure you know how to pray and fast. Then you are to find a quiet retreat somewhere, go there for whatever amount of time you can afford, and see what God will give you in that time."

We taught her how to pray, fast, write out the issues she was concerned with in a concise way, search the Bible for prescriptions on those issues, and keep a journal of what happened during the retreat. After seven days on retreat, she reported to the mentor with glowing insights on new direction in life.

We use a development plan form that provides space for (1) needs or goals, (2) assigned tasks, (3) required resources, (4) target date, and (5) comments. The mentor and mentoree have duplicate information, and a third copy is available for the program coordinator who monitors the relationship.

Periodic Meetings

Periodic meetings allow for the review of mentoree progress and the assignment of new tasks. Instruction is necessary, but it augments and does not take the place of association and relationship. American religion has too easily become an extension of secular educational techniques, and these will not suffice for a mentoring relationship. We remember that Jesus' technique was a twenty-four-hour association for three years with twelve men in order to change the world.

Mentors and mentorees commit themselves to keeping appointments, as a matter of contractual agreement. The frequency of meetings depends on the needs and goals the mentoree has. Some schedule appointments once a week for a period of two months, then only meet once a month or maintain phone contact every two months. One mentor met an average of twice a month with her two mentorees and sent reports on the meetings by the Internet to the program coordinator who, in turn, monitored the relationships and replied to the mentor within twenty-four hours of each report.

We remember that Jesus' technique was a twenty-four-hour association for three years with twelve men in order to change the world.

Reporting to the Program Coordinator

The coordinator requires periodic reports in order to monitor the progress of the mentoring relationship. The coordinator often serves as a safety value for both mentor and mentoree. Sometimes they intervene to keep the mentoree from demanding too much of the mentor's time, and they also have to be available to the mentoree if the mentor fails to keep appointments or becomes too possessive and demanding.

Mentoree Needs Met

The time comes when the mentoring contract is completed—needs and goals have met the satisfaction of mentor and mentoree. The mentor and mentoree are free to go their separate

ways. Both evaluate the progress made, the difficulties encountered, and the evidence for success. The value of having a
mentoring relationship that is issue- and task-oriented is that
visible accomplishments are evidence of growth and maturity.

The relationship between the two does not need to end. Our
experience has been that for most mentoring relationships, new
needs and goals emerge and extend the relationship for another
season, assuming the mentor is the right person for the next set
of needs or goals. If the mentor is not the right person, the coordinator can help select a new one to assist the mentoree.

Program Evaluation

Most of Jesus' parables have to do with stewardship and
accountability and require evaluation of behavior. Having been in
the institutional church for over fifty years, my experience has
been that there is a tendency for church managers to use impre-
cise "qualitative" or impressionistic measures of success rather
than put them in the form of more quantitative
measurable ones. It is common to assume that
matters of the spirit elude measurement.

*By agreeing before-
hand on a
performance
criterion—how a
task and its results
are measured—the
details of evaluation
are decided before
any action occurs.
The greatest benefit
of evaluation is for
the mentoree.*

Therefore, the mentor and mentoree early in
their relationship agree on how they will know
that a set of tasks will lead to a particular goal or
meet a particular need, and then they agree on
how they know that assigned tasks are completed.
A good way to measure results is to put them in
the form of behavior.

By agreeing beforehand on a performance
criterion—how a task and its results are
measured—the details of evaluation are decided
before any action occurs. The greatest benefit of
evaluation is for the mentoree.

Every task attempted and every obstruction
overcome increases the mentoree's hope. The
acquired habit strength, borne of all mentorees'
frustrations, discipline, suffering, disappointments, and temporary loss of vision, brings them to that place of *perfected purpose*,
and they, as Paul, can claim to have finished the course to which
they were called.

Eulogy to a Purpose-Driven Life

My frame was not hidden from Thee,
When I was made in secret,
And skillfully wrought in the depths of the earth.
Thine eyes have seen my unformed substance;
And in Thy book they were all written,
The days that were ordained for me,
When as yet there was not one of them.   *Psalm 139:15–16*

God sees not as man sees, for man looks at
The outward appearance, but the Lord looks at the heart.
Then Samuel took the horn of oil and anointed him . . . and
The Spirit of the Lord came mightily upon David from
That day forward.   *1 Samuel 16:7b, 13*

He raised up David to be their king, concerning whom
He also testified and said, 'I have found David
The son of Jesse, a man after My heart,
Who will do all My will.'   *Acts 13:22*

O Lord, my heart is not proud, nor my eyes haughty;
Nor do I involve myself in great matters,
Or in things too difficult for me.
Surely, I have composed and quieted my soul.   *Psalm 131:1–2*

Do not cast me off in the time of old age;
Do not forsake me when my strength fails.
And even when I am old and gray, O God,
Do not forsake me,
Until I declare Thy strength to this generation.   *Psalm 71:9, 18*

For David, after he had served the purpose of God
In his own generation,
Fell asleep, and was laid among his fathers . . .   *Acts 13:36*

Annotated Glossary on Types of Influence

Listed alphabetically are annotated definitions and comments on common ways people influence and guide others. While not exhaustive, these illustrate differences and present how mentoring fits into the mix. Seven areas include: (1) coaching, (2) counseling, (3) discipling, (4) mentoring (secular literature), (5) mentoring (religious literature), (6) role models, and (7) sponsors.

Coaching

William Hendricks on the relationship
(1) A trust relationship between coach and the person or the team coached
(2) A set of clarified expectations the coached person or team has of the coach
(3) Agreement on affirmed and acknowledged performance standards
(4) An environment of motivation and inspiration.[1]

Bob McCann on the coach
(1) He or she is a good listener.
(2) He or she has the ability to create a good working relationship with employees.
(3) He or she is a person with whom management can align itself.
(4) He or she is trustworthy.[2]

Margo Murray on the process
(1) Demonstrates the link between company culture and mentoring terminology
(2) Concerned primarily with productivity and competition
(3) Focuses on corporate team efforts rather than individual achievement.[3]

Counseling

Counseling has evolved considerably in recent years, and the changes warrant attention, particularly to show how recent trends begin to approximate some of the dynamics and circumstances connected with mentoring.

Jim Siress on corporate counseling
"Negative behavior, never confronted, never changes." This statement introduces the role of counseling in secular corporate structures, of which there are four phases:
(1) Get and give information
(2) Agree on performance standards
(3) Correct
(4) Refer the counselee to outside help.[4]

Counseling of this type, writes Siress, is for persons with problems. They may not fit into the corporate team as well as they should, or they may have a flaw preventing the team from functioning at its top task or morale levels. In the same manner as corporate coaching, counseling in corporate settings is first concerned with company productivity.

Jay Adams on confrontational counseling

The biblical counseling of Jay Adams from a generation ago is similar to what Siress describes.[5] Drawing from the *nouthetic*, or confrontational style of the apostle Paul, Adams advocates a highly directive approach, addressing sin, confession, forgiveness, and repentance. An example of confrontation and correction comes from the apostle Paul: "Let him who steals steal no longer; but rather let him labor, performing with his own hands what is good, in order that he may have something to share with him who has need" (Eph. 4:28). When first written, the direct, seemingly harsh confrontational emphasis on sin, as a premier cause of problems, had shock effect on the Christian counseling academy. Among the benefits, however, as remarked by Gary Collins, was a refocus on the role of God's once-for-all *judicial* forgiveness and the troubled person's need for repeated *parental* forgiveness.[6] The first assured the counselee of God's faithfulness and the sinner's continued membership in the heavenly family. The second assured a biblical way to reestablish relationship with others once broken by sin. At the heart of Adams's two-part model was "restoration subsequent to redemption." In recent years, restoration has increasingly become a ministry of the body of Christ, as seen in Collins and Crabb.

Gary Collins on counseling by people helpers

Gary Collins, important among the advocates of a new movement in Christian counseling, in 1991 and again in 1993, began to lay the basis for counseling and helping by others than professional counselors. "Everyday" (non-professional) Christians had a role to play in Collins's three-point approach. Accordingly, the Christian counselor is:

(1) a deeply committed, Spirit-guided (and Spirit-filled) servant of Jesus,
(2) who applies his or her God-given abilities, skills, training, knowledge, and insights,
(3) to the task of helping others move to personal wholeness, interpersonal competence, mental stability, and spiritual maturity.[7]

This definition includes believers who come from different theological perspectives, use different approaches to counseling, and have different levels of training and experience. At the time he wrote, Collins was president of the American Association of Christian Counselors and editor of *Christian Counseling Today* magazine. Both positions, therefore, had the effect of "speaking for many colleagues." The significant point was that the counseling profession leadership was divesting itself of a sole privilege of counseling and making it available to many others who expressed faith in Jesus Christ. The right to counsel went even further under the bold recommendations of Larry Crabb.

Larry Crabb on connecting

Larry Crabb joins a growing number who are discovering the remarkable healing resources abiding in the priesthood of all believers. In a groundbreaking proposal for his profession, Crabb takes the insights of Collins even further.

(1) God has placed extraordinary resources in us to heal us and our relationships.
(2) If these resources are released from within us, much good could be done that we have thought only trained specialists could accomplish.
(3) I believe that under the direction of the Holy Spirit these inner resources can move others toward maturity.
(4) I envision the church as connected people in small healing communities, where their connectedness depends on what they give to each other.[8]

Crabb describes for the counseling movement, therefore, what I described in the introduction as a new paradigm—a delegation of authority, within flatter church structures, to others. Under the moniker of "mentoring," pastoral eldering expands to others who bring Christians to their purposes of God. Crabb summarizes: "The community of God can be back in business as the major provider of soul care. The talking does not belong only to professionals. It also belongs to ordinary Christians."[9] The major difference between Crabb's connected people and the ones mentors serve as per this book is that Crabb's are within "healing communities," while the mentor is launching otherwise whole people to greater levels of proactive maturity and purpose.

Gary Collins on the soul search

Collins takes Crabb's concept of connecting communities beyond their healing function and addresses where I began this book—distinguishing between the authentic *agape* of God and humankind's efforts through *eros* to devise counterfeit pathways to God. Collins explores contemporary dead-end traps of non-biblical competing spiritualities, which are part of the new wave of postmodernism, and explores the more personal side of authentic spirituality in this age of stress and instability.[10]

Discipling

Ted Engstrom on discipling
(1) The disciple is an understudy who gives up his or her own will for the will of God the Father.
(2) The disciple lives a daily life of spiritual sacrifice for the glory of Christ.
(3) The disciple strives to be consistently obedient to the commands of the Master.[11]

Gordon MacDonald on current defects of maturing believers
MacDonald agrees with Engstrom and criticizes contemporary counter-methods in their efforts to mature believers. His critique describes what is true about much church-based discipling.

(1) Discipling happens in a classroom.
(2) Student certification is by diploma rather than approval from an overseer.
(3) The criterion for judgment rests upon knowledge rather than wisdom.
(4) The criterion for judgment rests upon achievement rather than character.[12]

Robert Coleman on the masterplan of evangelism

Coleman remains the classic statement on Jesus' method of evangelism. The method Jesus chose for proclaiming the message of the kingdom was through the making of disciples. Make disciples, Coleman says, and you evangelize. He sees Jesus discipling His men until they were reproducing themselves. He distinguishes the first half of the Lord's ministry, when elementary discipling occurred, and the more intense second half with its assignments, demand for accountability, and purpose-driven responsibility. The modern church, with its evangelistic emphasis, focuses primarily on the first half. MENTORING FOR AN AUDIENCE OF ONE emphasizes the second half. Coleman would agree with Engstrom's three points and, while recognizing them, would avoid the four deficiencies listed by MacDonald.[13]

Instruction

Six qualities define instruction.

(1) The transmission of information can be by teacher, books, radio, television, movies, video conferencing, audio and videocassettes, the Internet, or compact discs.
(2) With the exception of instruction by a live teacher, instruction is available anywhere and at anytime.
(3) With the exception of instruction by a live teacher or video-conferencing, there is no face-to-face contact between student and sources of instruction.
(4) Interaction with a live teacher is formal, didactic, and from a distance.
(5) Evaluation occurs primarily by written examination.
(6) Accountability and changed behavior are applied arbitrarily.

Mentoring in Secular Settings

Rotarian *magazine on establishing balance*

(1) Mentoring balances personal accessibility and oversight with delegation of responsibility to the mentored person.
(2) Mentoring balances familiarity with personal knowledge of the mentoree while continuing to be a responsible boss.
(3) Mentoring proves by action that the mentor is trustworthy.
(4) Mentoring balances sympathy for the demanding requirements expected of a mentoree with the hard taskmaster role of the mentor.[14]

Chip R. Bell on creating the right environment

(1) The mentor pushes employees with high expectations.
(2) The mentor listens dramatically to show that the mentoree's input is valued and makes a difference.
(3) The mentor is true to his or her word, letting actions be consistent with words.
(4) The mentor celebrates the employee's successes with deliberate reference to the actions that resulted in the success.
(5) The mentor encourages growth by regular acquisition of new skills.[15]

Margo Murray on process and expectations

(1) Facilitated mentoring is a deliberate pairing of a more skilled or experienced person with a lesser-skilled or experienced one, with the agreed-upon goal of having the lesser-skilled person grow and develop specific competencies.[16]

(2) Mentorees must be low maintenance and high impact, know their purposes, and be able to express them or already be in pursuit of them.[17]

Mentoring in Religious Settings

Hans Finzel on reasons for too few leaders as mentors

(1) Inadequate training and mentoring to become leaders

(2) Overemphasis of pastors on how to do ministry

(3) Absence of training pastors on how to lead others.[18]

Kevin Miller on hindrances to leader development

(1) Inappropriate emphasis on classes, seminars, and programs

(2) Avoidance of the Jesus method: day-to-day mentoring of students who watched and did.[19]

Bobb Biehl on forming the mentoring relationship

(1) Mentor turns to mentoree and says, "I love you, believe in you, and want to help you succeed. I want to make my experience and resources available to you in any way I can to become all that God wants you to be."

(2) The mentoring relationship is born the moment a person with experience asks a less-experienced person what his or her priorities are, how the mentor can help and, of course, receives an affirmative response.[20]

Howard and William Hendricks on the matrix
of God-generated influences

(1) The matrix

Our membership with other Christians is in perpetuity in the sense we forever belong to the body of Christ. Our relationships are not always to the same people. One's pattern of growth results from a matrix of God-generated influences to help believers mature in Christ: the Word, the home, the local church, experiences in ministry, crises and conflicts, books, tapes and conferences, and others. The mentor, as a seasoned believer and leader, plays a vital role in this maturity matrix. "Remember your leaders, who spoke the word of God to you. Consider the outcome of their way of life and imitate their faith." (Heb. 13:7). "What we need are relationships with people who know Christ (experientially) and can help us know Him at our point of need."[21]

(2) Mentoring is a problem-solving and goal-oriented activity

The best mentors provide genuine growth and change; provide a model to follow; help the mentoree reach goals more efficiently; play a key role in God's pattern for growth; and have an influence that benefits others in the mentoree's circle of associates.[22]

(3) The mentor as role model

The mentor provides close supervision on special projects, individualized help in many areas—discipline, encouragement, correction, confrontation, and a calling to accountability. The mentor is a role model in the sense that Jesus Christ was the perfect model of godliness. Philip asked Jesus, "Show us the Father," to which Jesus replied, "Anyone who has seen me has seen the Father" (John 14:8–9). Peter echoed that we should follow in the steps of Jesus (1 Pet. 2:21), and Paul drew attention to himself saying that "as I follow Christ, so you follow my example" (1 Cor. 11:1; Phil. 3:17; 4:9).[23]

Role Models

(1) Have a social or psychological impact on someone because of exceptional qualities
(2) May be near or far, but are not expected to interact with admirers
(3) May not know or be personally known by the admiring person
(4) May be an example to more than one person at a time
(5) Do not expect a change in the behavior of admirers

Sponsors

(1) Investment in favored person(s)
(2) May be near or far, but are not expected to interact with sponsoree
(3) May be anonymous to sponsoree and sponsoree may be unknown to sponsor
(4) May be sponsor to more than one person at a time
(5) Do not demand a change in the sponsoree, but there is expectation of change in the sponsoree because of social or economic investment
(6) May withdraw support at any time.

PERFECTINGPURPOSE ™

First Access International, Inc. is one of several national management-consulting companies founded over thirty years ago by Dr. Charles Oakes. He currently serves as FAI's CEO and chairman of the board. The company's staff of independent contractors applies biblical principles and established management practices to serve religious organizations and for-profit businesses.

FAI's trademark PerfectingPurpose™ expresses its mission to assist people in reaching their God-given purposes at the level of performance of which they are capable. This is accomplished in two ways.

First, mentors are trained to carry out the PerfectingPurpose™ mission and design and develop self-sustaining mentoring programs as part of a client's larger leadership development efforts. FAI conducts Intensive Training Seminars on the client's site. Churches benefit when seminar graduates become leaders in their own right and help lighten the load of salaried staff. FAI also helps individuals discover their purposeful pursuits and gives them strategies for carrying these out. A major benefit of this for businesses has been to encourage personal aspirations of employees in order to enhance overall job performance. MENTORING FOR AN AUDIENCE OF ONE and its operations manual are the pivotal publications for this effort.

FAI also assists older adults in establishing later-life purposes. Two-day weekend retreats meet many of the needs of churches' senior ministry programs. The retreats also satisfy some of the goals of a corporation's preretirement counseling programs. When offered to individuals or churches, FAI helps resurrect, reestablish, and plan efforts to activate years of a person's accumulated natural skills and spiritual gifts that result in a more satisfying and proactive lifestyle. Many older adults have discovered new purpose and determination from these programs and from the book that articulates them—*Working the Gray Zone,* also by Oakes.

For more information see www.perfectingpurpose.com; e-mail: Oakes5@home.com; call: 615-731-5999; fax: 615-731-7601.

NOTES

Introduction

1. James Dale Davidson and Lord William Rees-Mogg, *The Sovereign Individual* (New York, N.Y.: Simon and Schuster, 1997), 84–87, 102–7.

2. Colonel V. Doner, *The Samaritan Strategy* (Brentwood, Tenn.: Wolgemuth & Hyatt, 1988), 43–59.

3. Herbert Schlossberg, *Idols for Destruction* (Wheaton, Ill.: Crossway Books, 1990), 235–39.

4. Donald W. McCullough, *The Trivialization of God: The Dangerous Illusion of a Manageable Deity* (Colorado Springs, Colo.: NavPress, 1995), 27–51.

5. George Gilder, "Over the Paradigm Cliff," *ASAP* (February 1997): 29.

6. Jack Hayford, *Pastors of Promise: Pointing to Character and Hope As the Keys to Fruitful Shepherding* (Ventura, Calif.: Regal Books, 1997).

7. Charles Simpson, *Challenge to Care* (Ann Arbor, Mich.: Servant Publications, 1986).

8. Bobb Biehl, *Mentoring: Confidence in Finding a Mentor and Becoming One* (Nashville, Tenn.: Broadman and Holman, 1996).

9. Howard and William Hendricks, *As Iron Sharpens Iron* (Chicago, Ill.: Moody, 1995).

10. Mike Bellah, *Baby Boomer Believers* (Wheaton, Ill.: Tyndale House Publishers, 1988).

11. Mario Murillo, *Fresh Fire* (Danville, Calif.: Anthony Douglas Publishing, 1991), 129–35.

12. John Seel, in *Regeneration Quarterly*, as quoted in *Intercessors for America Newsletter* 25:4 (April 1998): 3.

13. Elliot Carlson and Leah Glasheen, "MIT futurist sees 'connected nation,'" *AARP Bulletin* 39:4 (April 1998): 1, 12.

14. George Barna, *The Second Coming of the Church* (Nashville, Tenn.: Word, 1998), 65, 180.

15. John Naisbitt and Patricia Aburdene, *Megatrends 2000* (New York, N. Y.: Morrow, 1990), 118, 270.

16. Peter F. Drucker, *The New Realities* (New York, N.Y.: Harper and Row, 1989), 261–63.

17. For an excellent essay on this topic, see Kurt Reizler, *Man, Mutable and Immutable—The Fundamental Structure of Social Life* (Chicago, Ill.: Regnery Co., 1950).

Chapter 1

1. Theologians Thomas Oden and Christopher Hall edit a series entitled *Ancient Christian Commentary on Scripture* (Downers Grove, Ill.: Intervarsity Press, 1998). Oden and Hall publish the commentaries on Scripture of patristic fathers who wrote over a seven-century period from Clement of Rome through A.D. 750. Some reviewers suggest this series provides a fresh insight into commentaries that have been long neglected except by scholars located in institutions with rare literary collections.

2. J. I. Packer, et al., *The Bible Almanac* (Nashville, Tenn.: Thomas Nelson Co., 1980), 455.

3. W. E. Vine, Merrill F. Unger, and William White Jr., *Vine's Complete Expository Dictionary of Old and New Testament Words* (Nashville, Tenn.: Thomas Nelson Co., 1985), 108–9.

4. An outstanding theological work of the early twentieth century is Anders Nygren's *Agape and Eros*, translated by Philip S. Watson (The Westminster Press, published in one volume, 1953, and various parts published in Great Britain by S. P. C. K. House, between 1932 and 1939).

5. Bob Mumford of LifeChangers, Inc., Raleigh, North Carolina, has formulated the most definitive contemporary statement on the *eros* and *agape* paradigm. It appeared in the late 1990s in audio and video formats under the title "Unshared Love." It has been revised, still in video format, and republished by LifeWay, Inc., Nashville, Tennessee, under the title "The Agape Road."

Chapter 2

1. General references used for this section are Charles Simpson, general editor, *The Covenant and the Kingdom* (Kent, England: Sovereign World, Ltd., 1995), 133–34; Bob Mumford, *The Difference Between the Church and the Kingdom*, (Raleigh, N.C.: Life Changers, nd); George Eldon Ladd, *The Gospel of the Kingdom*, (Grand Rapids, Mich.: William B. Eerdmans Publishing Co., 1959, The Paternoster Press); and Bernard Ramm, *Protestant Biblical Interpretation*, third revised edition, (Grand Rapids, Mich.: Baker Book House, 1970), 280–81.

Chapter 3

1. For an excellent discussion on this, see Dan McCartney and Charles Clayton, *Let the Reader Understand—A Guide to Interpreting and Applying the Bible* (Wheaton, Ill.: A Bridgepoint Book, Victor Books/SP Publications, Inc., 1994), chapter 10: "Scripture and Guidance."

2. John and Paula Sanford, *The Elijah Task—A Call to Today's Prophets* (Plainfield, N.J.: Logos, 1977), 61.

3. Ibid.

4. An excellent essay on this topic is by theologian Rousas J. Rushdoony, *Politics of Guilt and Pity* (Fairfax, Va.: Thoburn Press, 1978).

5. Robert Coleman, *The Masterplan of Evangelism* (Grand Rapids, Mich.: Fleming H. Revell, 1993), 50.

Chapter 4

1. Edmund Sinnott, *Biology of the Spirit* (New York, N.Y.: The Viking Press, 1955).

2. Joannie M. Schrof, "No Whining," *U.S. News and World Report* (14 July 1997): 48–55.

3. *Intercessors for America Newsletter* 25:6 (June 1998): 1.

4. Charles Henry Mackintosh, *The Mackintosh Treasury* (Neptune, N.J.: Loizeaux Brothers, 1976), 786–87.

5. Henri M. Nouwen and Kenneth E. Bailey have provided graphic pictures of the characters involved in the parable, with particular attention being given to the father (*The Return of the Prodigal Son*, New York, N.Y.: Image Books, Doubleday, 1992; and *Poet and Peasant and Through Peasant Eyes*, Grand Rapids, Mich.: William B. Eerdmans Publishing Co., combined edition, 1976, 158ff).

6. Packer, 192.
7. I am indebted to Dr. Duane Christensen for this clarification and its value for this study.
8. Vine, 325.

Chapter 5
1. Gordon MacDonald, foreword, in Ted Engstorm, *The Fine Art of Mentoring* (Brentwood, Tenn.: Wolgemuth & Hyatt, 1989): ix-x.
2. Coleman, 49–50.
3. Vine, 692.
4. Ibid., 228. Debate exists whether John was actually addressing three different age groups—children, young men, and fathers, or addressing persons of varying degrees of spiritual maturity. Both seem likely to be true.
5. R. C. Sproul, *The Holiness of God* (Wheaton, Ill.: Tyndale House Publishers, 1998), 157–71.
6. Vine, 204.
7. The general reference on envy is Helmut Schoeck, *Envy: A Theory of Social Behavior* (Indianapolis, Ind.: Liberty Press, 1969).

Chapter 6
1. Aaron Ben-Ze'ev, "Emotions and Morality," *Journal of Value Inquiry*. 0:1–18 1997, Kluwer Academic Publishers, the Netherlands. See also by the same author, *Subtlety of Emotions* (Cambridge, Mass.: MIT Press, 2000).

Chapter 7
1. Barna, 36.
2. I. Howard Marshall, ed., et al., *New Bible Dictionary*, Third Edition (Downers Grove, Ill.: Intervarsity Press, 1996) 954–55.
3. Barna, 36, 38.
4. Steven R. Covey, *The 7 Habits of Highly Effective People* (New York, N.Y.: Simon and Schuster, 1989), 101.
5. Barna, 108–10, with modifications.
6. Nanus, 12–15.
7. Barna, 114–18.
8. Ralph Mattson, *Visions of Grandeur* (Chicago, Ill.: Praxis/Moody, 1994).
9. Ibid., 163.

Chapter 8
1. C. S. Lewis, *God in the Dock* (Grand Rapids, Mich.: William B. Eerdmans, 1970), 96.
2. A personal testimony to the efficacy of parental involvement occurred when my wife and I, during our two sons' grammar school years, recruited evangelical Christians to be candidates for elected positions on local parent-teachers organization (PTO) boards. We campaigned throughout our county to mobilize the Christian vote, and every Christian candidate won election to fill every vacancy in every school. The kingdom had arrived. This occurred at a time when the local school board had just hired a new high school principal, a Christian, to route out the local drug culture. Within one year, with the help of newly elected PTO members, the school was clean, and the principal received a prolonged standing ovation by students at the annual convocation.

3. Rushdoony.

4. Marvin Olasky, *The Tragedy of American Compassion* (Washington, D.C.: Regnery Publishing, Inc., 1992).

5. Thomas Sowell, *Inside American Education* (New York, N.Y.: The Free Press, 1993).

6. Doner.

Chapter 9

1. Margo Murray, *Beyond the Myths and Magic of Mentoring* (San Francisco, Calif.: Jossey-Bass Publishers, 1991), 122–23.

2. S. Everitt and M. Murray-Hicks, "Models, Mentors, and Sponsors for Managers," Presented at the National Society for Performance and Instructional Conference, Montreal, Canada, 1981, as cited in Margo Murray, *Beyond the Myths and Magic of Mentoring*, 107–12, 118.

3. Marshall, 305–6.

4. *Tanakh—The Holy Scriptures* (Philadelphia, Penn.: The Jewish Publication Society, 1985), 1219.

5. Ibid., 1228.

6. George Barna, *The Frog in the Kettle* (Ventura, Calif.: Regal Books, A Division of Gospel Light, 1990), 207.

Chapter 10

1. George Barna, *Marketing the Church* (Colorado Springs, Colo.: NavPress, 1988), 79–92.

2. Guy Kawasaki, *Selling the Dream* (New York, N.Y.: Harper Business, 1991), 3–14.

3. Burt Nanus, *Visionary Leadership* (San Francisco, Calif.: Jossey-Bass, 1992), 3–22.

4. Tom Peters, *Thriving on Chaos* (New York, N.Y.: A Borzoi Book, Knopf, 1987), 399.

5. James C. Collins and Jerry I. Porris, *Built to Last* (New York, N.Y.: Harper-Collins, 1994).

6. John Piper, "There is No Greater Satisfaction," *Mission Frontiers* 20:1–2 (January–February 1998): 12–13.

7. Charles V. Simpson, "The Ultimate Vision," *Christian Conquest* (Spring 1997): 2–5.

8. Kevin Miller, *Leadership Journal* 17:4.

9. Tom Brown, "On the Edge with Jim Collins," *Industry Week* (5 October 1992): 12–20.

10. James Rutz, *Open Church* (Auburn, Maine: The Seedsowers, 1992).

11. Ralph Neighbor, *Where Do We Go From Here?* (Houston, Tex.: TOUCH Publications, 1990).

12. William A. Beckham, *The Second Reformation* (Houston, Tex.: TOUCH Publications, 1995).

13. Alexander Strauch, *Biblical Eldership—An Urgent Call to Restore Biblical Church Leadership* (revised and expanded, Littleton, Colo.: Lewis and Roth Publishers, 1995).

Appendix

1. William Hendricks, ed., *Coaching, Mentoring, and Managing* (Franklin Lakes, N.J.: Career Press, 1996), 73.

2. Bob McCann, pamphlet, n.d., (Sacramento, Calif.: The Wendling Group).

3. Murray, 11.

4. Hendricks, 157.

5. Hendricks, 157.

6. Jay Adams, *The Christian Counselor's Manual* (Grand Rapids, Mich.: Baker Book House, 1973), 14–17.

7. Gary R. Collins, *The Biblical Basis of Christian Counseling for People Helpers* (Colorado Spring, Colo.: NavPress, 1993), 141.

8. Ibid., 21.

9. Larry Crabb, *Connecting* (Nashville, Tenn.: Word Publishing, 1997), xiv.

10. Ibid., 202.

11. Gary R. Collins, *The Soul Search: A Spiritual Journey to Authentic Intimacy with God* (Nashville, Tenn.: Thomas Nelson Co.).

12. Ted Engstrom, *The Fine Art of Mentoring* (Brentwood, Tenn.: Wolgemuth & Hyatt, 1989), ix–x.

13. Ibid.

14. Coleman.

15. *Rotarian* (March, 1997): 20–23.

16. Chip R. Bell, *Security Management* (January, 1998): 26, 33.

17. Murray, 63–66.

18. Ibid., 118–130.

19. Hans Finzel, *The Top Ten Mistakes Leaders Make*, as quoted by Helen Lee in *Christianity Today*, 1995.

20. Kevin Miller.

21. Bobb Biehl, xiv, 26.

22. Hendrix and Hendrix, 25–31.

23. Ibid.

24. Ibid., 129.

BIBLIOGRAPHY

Barna, George. *The Second Coming of the Church*. Nashville, Tenn.: Word Publishing, 1998.

Beckham, William A. *The Second Reformation*. Houston, Tex.: TOUCH Publications, 1995.

Beeson, Ray, and Ranelda Mack Hunsicker. *The Hidden Price of Greatness*. Wheaton, Ill.: Tyndale House Publishers, Inc., 1991.

Biehl, Bobb. *Mentoring: Confidence in Finding a Mentor and Becoming One*. Nashville, Tenn.: Broadman and Holman, 1996.

Coleman, Robert E. *The Master Plan of Evangelism, 30th Anniversary Edition*. Grand Rapids, Mich.: Fleming H. Revell, 1993.

Downer, Phil. *Eternal Impact: Investing in the Lives of Men*. Eugene, Ore.: Harvest House Publishers, 1997.

Dowgiewicz, Mike and Sue. *Pastoring by Elders*. Colorado Springs, Colo.: Empowerment Press, 1998.

Farah, Charles. *From the Pinnacle of the Temple*. Plainfield, N.J.: Logos International, 1979.

Garber, Steven. *The Fabric of Faithfulness*. Downers Grove, Ill.: InterVarsity Press, 1996.

Hayford, Jack W. *Pastors of Promise: Pointing to Character and Hope As the Keys to Fruitful Shepherding*. Ventura, Calif.: Regal Books, 1997.

Hendricks, Howard and William. *As Iron Sharpens Iron*. Chicago, Ill.: Moody Press, 1995.

Hendricks, William, Ed. *Coaching, Mentoring and Managing*. Franklin Lakes, N.J.: Career Press, 1996.

Hunt, Susan. *Spiritual Mothering: The Titus 2 Model for Women Mentoring Women*. Wheaton, Ill.: Crossway Books, 1993.

Krallman, Gunter. *Mentoring for Mission*. Second Edition. Hong Kong: Jensco, Ltd., 1994.

Ladd, George E. *Crucial Questions about the Kingdom of God*. Grand Rapids, Mich.: William B. Eerdmans Publishing Co., 1952.

———. *The Gospel of the Kingdom*. Grand Rapids, Mich.: William B. Eerdmans Publishing Company, 1977.

Mattson, Ralph T. *Visions of Grandeur*. Chicago, Ill.: Moody Press, 1994.

McCullough, Donald W. *The Trivialization of God*. Colorado Springs, Colo.: NavPress Publishing Group, 1995.

Mowrer, O. Hobart. *Learning Theory and Behavior*. New York, N.Y.: John Wiley & Sons, Inc., 1960.

Murray, Margo. *Beyond the Myths and Magic of Mentoring*. San Francisco, Calif.: Jossey-Bass Publishers, 1991.

Nanus, Burt. *Visionary Leadership*. San Francisco, Calif.: Jossey-Bass Publishers, 1992.

Nygren, Anders. *Agape and Eros*. Translated by Philip S. Watson. Philadelphia, Pa.: The Westminster Press, 1953.

Otto, Donna. *The Gentle Art of Mentoring*. Eugene, Ore.: Harvest House Publishers, 1997.

Rushdoony, Rousas John. *Thy Kingdom Come*. Fairfax, Va.: Thoburn Press, 1978.

Schlossberg, Herbert. *Idols for Destruction*. Wheaton, Ill.: Crossway Books, 1990.

Schoeck, Helmut. *Envy*. Indianapolis, Ind.: Liberty Press, 1966.

Simpson, Charles. *The Challenge to Care*. Ann Arbor, Mich.: Servant Publications, 1986.

Simpson, Charles. *The Covenant and the Kingdom*. Kent, England: Sovereign World, Ltd., 1995.

Sproul, R. C. *The Holiness of God*. Second Edition. Wheaton, Ill.: Tyndale House Publishers, Inc., 1998.

Stanley, J. Robert Clinton. *Connecting the Mentoring Relationships You Need to Succeed in Life*. Colorado Springs, Colo.: NavPress Publishing Group, 1992.

Strauch, Alexander. *Biblical Eldership*. Littleton, Colo.: Lewis and Roth Publishers, 1995.

ABOUT THE AUTHOR

Author, academician, management consultant, gerontologist, and entrepreneur Charles Oakes spent forty years in the secular marketplace and fifty-five years studying the Bible for its relevance to the affairs of everyday life. Dr. Oakes received graduate training at the University of California, Berkeley, and Stanford and Emory Universities. He has been on the teaching and research faculties of the University of Tennessee College of Medicine and Duke University Medical Center. This book represents an integration of his training as a behavioral scientist and management consultant to arrive at a practical application of biblical mentoring, and derives from many years of having mentored men and women in religious and secular settings.

Dr. Oakes developed and now directs the mentoring program at the seven-thousand-member Christ Church in Nashville, Tennessee, and travels nationally training mentors and establishing mentoring programs in churches and businesses. More information about his programs is available from www.perfecting-purpose.com.

Dr. Oakes is the author of *Working the Gray Zone*, also published by Providence House Publishers, as well as *Foundations for Practical Gerontology* and *The Walking Patient and the Health Care Crisis*.

Carolyn, his wife, is trained as a medical social worker and geriatric case manager and has been a constant companion and colleague in business and professional pursuits as well as in guiding their two sons, Mark and Brad, who also have successful business careers. Carolyn is a nationally certified instructor in water aerobics and combines this challenge with Tai Chi for older adults.